An International View of True and Fair Accounting

Since its genesis in the 1947 Companies Act, 'a true and fair view' has produced much debate among professionals. In this book, Parker and Nobes bring together the explanatory and often contentious opinions of key international accountants and lawyers for the first time.

By including documents that have shaped international usage of that convention, Parker and Nobes provide a useful analysis of the full meaning and effect of a true and fair view.

Considered a 'will-o-the-wisp' subject by most academic writers, the concept of 'a true and fair view' remains pivotal in much current accounting practice. Nobes and Parker grasp the nettle and attempt to clarify what international opinion has concluded about this central accounting issue.

R.H. Parker is Professor of Accounting at the University of Exeter. **C.W. Nobes** is Coopers & Lybrand Professor of Accounting at the University of Reading.

Routledge series on international accounting and finance

Edited by C.W. Nobes

An International View of True and Fair Accounting

R.H. Parker and C.W. Nobes

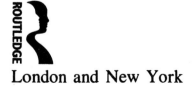
London and New York

First published 1994
by Routledge
11 New Fetter Lane, London EC4P 4EE

Simultaneously published in the USA and Canada
by Routledge
29 West 35th Street, New York, NY 10001

Reprinted 1995

© 1994 R.H. Parker and C.W. Nobes

Typeset in Times by Mews Photosetting, Beckenham, Kent

Printed and bound in Great Britain by Antony Rowe Ltd,
Chippenham, Wiltshire

British Library Cataloguing in Publication Data
A catalogue record for this book is available from the British Library

Library of Congress Cataloguing in Publication Data
A catalogue record for this book is available from the Library of Congress

ISBN 0–415–11463–2

Contents

Figures and tables

Foreword
The True and Fair View –
A Standard-Setter's Perspective

The overriding requirement that annual financial statements should give a true and fair view underlies the structure of accounting standard-setting in the United Kingdom and the approach of the Accounting Standards Board (ASB) to its task. As a standard-setter, the Board aims to establish and improve standards of financial accounting and reporting for the benefit of users, preparers and auditors of financial information. Broadly speaking, its objective is to move financial reporting forward to meet the legitimate aspirations of users of accounts for information to enable them to assess both the effects of a company's interaction with its trading environment and its financial strength at the end of that period. These aspirations, however, must be limited by a need to match the costs of producing the information against the benefits resulting from its disclosure. The presentation of financial information, therefore, entails a trade-off involving commercial sensitivity, costs of production, relevance and reliability. All these matters weigh heavily with the Board, as does the need to move in an evolutionary, not in a revolutionary, way. Breaking the mould may be desirable to some commentators on accounting issues, but too sudden a shock to the financial reporting system may leave users and preparers unsure of their bearings as familiar markers disappear and the frame of reference is lost. The true and fair view reflects the broad consensus of the financial community on the amount, nature and form of presentation of information at a particular point in time. It is an ambulatory concept changing gradually over the years as further information is required and new accounting practices develop.

The concept, as I have written elsewhere, is necessary, first, because no matter how skilled the standard-setter or the law-maker, ultimately situations arise that are not catered for by regulation or are symptomatic of the changing times and reveal that particular provisions of law and standards have become outdated. Second, attempts may be made by a few of those presenting financial information to play at the edges of the rules and create an effect that was certainly not intended by the original draftsman. The true and fair view puts these matters in perspective. Ultimately no matter what standards or laws exist, the true and fair view acts, as Professor David Flint has written (1982), as a safety valve remedying the deficiencies of prescription and ensuring that departures from the recognized regulations and practices should only be permissible when they do fairly reflect what has happened to a company.

In recent years, attempts have been made to use the true and fair view with regressive effect to give a stamp of approval to questionable new practices. As an auditor, I had difficulty in qualifying a dubious practice which had been accepted by two or three major companies and two or three other major auditors. Where such an accounting treatment was not specifically prohibited by a provision of law or standards it would be deemed by accountants and lawyers to be 'accepted practice' and pass into the corpus of practices encompassed by the true and fair view – a situation which became known as the 'creeping crumple'! Changes in law or accounting standards would then be necessary to rectify the position. Some of these poor practices, in my opinion, failed to take account of the true and fair view and arose because of an obsession with the letter (or absence of the letter) rather than the spirit of regulations – to some of us the acceptance of such practices and attitudes was a failure of professionalism.

The tide turned with the establishment in 1990 of the new procedures for setting accounting standards. As indicated in the Opinion of Miss Mary Arden QC, now the Honourable Mrs Justice Arden (1993; see Appendix IV), the statutory foundation for the new procedures, including enforcement, and the extension of the responsibility for standard-setting from the accounting profession to a wider body also including representatives of Government, business and the financial community, makes it likely that the Board will have more success than its predecessor in ensuring that the spirit of its standards is applied in practice.

A further weapon is available to the Board to enable it to react to the unfortunate choices of accounting treatments that led to the regressive use of true and fair. The Urgent Issues Task Force (UITF) can now ban such precedents at very short notice without the inevitable delay required to produce a new accounting standard. The maintenance of the principle of true and fair, therefore, is being assisted at the sharp edge by the Task Force members, those practitioners and finance directors who meet problems on a day-to-day basis and who are well qualified to pass judgement on the merits of accounting schemes. Bad practices are likely to be banned and the timely touch on the tiller prevents reporting practice from sailing into dangerous waters.

Much of the detail of accounting standards should hardly be needed. Several standards that the Board will issue will undoubtedly be of the nature of 'negative' standards, stamping out practices that many may believe should never have occurred in the first place. Others, however, will be required to deal with situations where there are genuine differences of opinion and a standard rule has to be adopted. Ultimately, standards can only deal with part of a problem. The Board's aim is to produce what we loosely term '80 per cent standards', dealing with the core 80 per cent of the problems and leaving the remaining 20 per cent of the ancillary issues to professional judgement, tempered by the spirit of the true and fair view. If, of course, that trust is abused, the Board or the Urgent Issues Task Force will be forced to intervene and the remaining issues, which previously had not been deemed to be so important, will then have to be considered. Such a development will lead inevitably towards a rule book and an increase in prescription. This, to my mind, is still avoidable but only on condition that those minority of preparers who wish to look for loopholes in accounting regulation, and auditors who hitherto have been willing to concur if there is no rule to oppose a particular practice, revert to the consideration of the proper spirit and objective of financial reporting. If they do not then their competitors inevitably will feel obliged to follow suit until the practice has ultimately to be banned. The number of accounting standards and UITF pronouncements lies outside the control of the Board and the Task Force. Ideally these committees should be dealing with new situations where there is doubt about the requisite accounting. They certainly should not be dealing with the inability of a few members of the profession to defend the overriding principle of financial reporting.

I have long been a believer in the supremacy of the true and fair view. I can understand the need to depart from an accounting standard in unusual situations – provided genuine special circumstances exist. The true and fair view requires a fair reflection of what has happened to an entity and this must not be distorted by the inadequacies of accounting regulation to describe what actually happened.

I am delighted that my long-standing friends, Professor Parker and Professor Nobes, have produced this much overdue book on the international assessments of true and fair. They have long researched this subject in which they too have a special interest. Readers will see the different views emerging and be able to re-examine the arguments of the past. Yet for me the central message would appear to be that the evolving nature of true and fair still predominates. Although there have been attempts in various countries to equate true and fair with accounting prescription, in my view this is doomed to failure. There is more to life and accounting than a series of rules. There must be a meaning, some overriding objective: in financial reporting it is the true and fair view.

Sir David Tweedie
Chairman, Accounting Standards Board

Preface

The purpose of this book is to explore the 'true and fair view' which is, for many Commonwealth and European countries, a central but mysterious feature of financial reporting. The true and fair view requirement is, at once, overriding and undefined. Like the English language, it had small beginnings but has spread over large areas of the globe. It is to be found not only in its native habitat of Great Britain but in Australasia, parts of South East Asia and Africa, and most of Europe, having even leapt across the frontiers of the European Community (EC). It has had to adapt to its new habitats but is still viewed as outlandish in some of them.

The authors have drawn up for this book an extensive Bibliography on writings in English on 'true and fair'. This does not, of course, include the (generally recent) literature on the subject in continental European languages. Nor does it include the literature on the distinctively different North American concept of fair presentation. The first chapter of this book is an analysis of the contents of the bibliography. This traces developments and stresses important papers.

The book also brings together four of the authors' papers on true and fair, concerning particularly, the UK (Chapters 2 and 3), the European Community (Chapter 4) and Australia (Chapter 5). The work on the two UK papers was assisted by a grant from the Research Board of the Institute of Chartered Accountants in England and Wales. These papers examine the meaning in practice of true and fair to directors and auditors of large UK companies.

The next two papers examine the spread of the true and fair view requirement through the EC due to harmonization, and the questioning by Australians of their true and fair legacy.

The book's final contribution is to bring together five brief writings of great relevance to true and fair. Appendix I reprints a paper from a Dutch journal in which Steve Zeff looks at the connection between

UK, US and Dutch wordings in the area of true and fair. Appendices II to IV contain English and Scottish legal counsels' opinions on the importance of the true and fair requirement and its relationship to other provisions of the law and to accounting standards. Appendix V contains Abstract 7 of the UK's Urgent Issues Task Force.

For writing the Foreword, we are grateful to David Tweedie, who has often marched into battle under the banner of truth and fairness. We are also grateful to the Research Committee of the Institute of Chartered Accountants of Scotland and the Research Board of the Institute of Chartered Accountants in England and Wales for sponsoring this book. We acknowledge the editors of several journals and the Accounting Standards Board for allowing us to reprint material.

R.H. Parker
University of Exeter

C.W. Nobes
University of Reading

1 What They Say About True and Fair

A Survey of the English-language Literature

ORIGINS

The legal requirement for UK balance sheets and profit and loss accounts to 'give a true and fair view' dates from the Companies Act 1947 (consolidated into the Companies Act 1948), replacing earlier references in Companies Acts from 1844 onwards to 'full and fair' and 'true and correct' (Chastney, 1975, ch. 2; Nobes and Parker, 1991, Appendix A; for pre-1844 usage see Chambers and Wolnizer, 1991).[1] The wording of the Acts was changed as a result of a memorandum submitted to the Cohen Committee on Company Law Amendment in 1944 by the Institute of Chartered Accountants in England and Wales (ICAEW).

No detailed reasons were suggested for the change. When asked by the Committee whether in the then existing requirement for accounts to be 'true and correct' there was a difference between 'true' and 'correct', the representatives of the ICAEW, Sir Harold Howitt and Mr (later Sir) Thomas Robson merely stated:

> We have suggested the change to 'true and fair'. We discussed it among ourselves and felt that the word 'fair' is probably better than 'correct'.
>
> (Minutes of Evidence, 25 February 1944, Q. 6704)

In response to a later question, Robson stated:

> The reason is that some people feel that in dealing with matters of estimate, such as one has to deal with in accounts, the word 'correct' is rather too rigid; for example, depreciation of fixed assets only represents the best estimate that one can make of the amount which should be provided; some other person might take a different view. It might be as near the right figure as one's own estimate. We felt that Parliament was really asking to be assured that the accounts had been drawn up to show a fair picture which was

less rigid but conveyed the same kind of general impression as 'correct'.

(ibid., Q. 6833)

A leading article in *The Accountant* (1944, p. 2) commented:

> The word 'correct' has always been too strong because it implies that there is one view which is 'correct' as against all others which are incorrect. In published accounts there is no standard of absolute truth and the Institute's suggested amendment would recognise that the presentation of the figures can be only that which is, in the personal opinion of the auditor, a 'fair view'.

Sir Russell Kettle, the one accountant member of the Committee, and the adviser to the Government on the implementation of the Committee's accounting recommendations in the 1947 amending Act, provided the following explanation:

> I wish to emphasise the importance of the term 'fair' in relation to the form of presentation of accounts. We must avoid the danger of over-elaboration of the balance sheet and profit and loss account at the expense of clarity by burdening them with too much detail, in contrast to the opposite extreme of paucity and ambiguity of information which characterised many accounts in the past. A true and fair view implies that all statutory and other essential information is not only available but is presented in a form in which it can be properly and readily appreciated.

(Kettle, 1950, p. 117)

EARLY DISCUSSION IN THE UK

Until the late 1960s the true and fair requirement appears to have been accepted in the UK without much debate. The Jenkins Report on Company Law Amendment of 1962 reported its opinion that:

> The formula 'true and fair' seems to us satisfactory as an indication of the required standard [of disclosure], while it makes for certainty to prescribe specific information which the law regards as the minimum necessary for the purpose of attaining that standard. It seems to be generally understood that the accounts may not lawfully omit any of the information specified in the Eighth Schedule, without the authority of the Board of Trade; but we doubt if it is always appreciated that accounts which comply strictly with the requirements of the Eighth Schedule (and of sections 196 and 197) may still fail to give the true

and fair view required by the Act, although we think this is the effect of section 149(3), which provides that the duty to give the detailed information required by the Eighth Schedule is without prejudice to the general duty to give a true and fair view.

(Cmnd. 1749, 1962, para. 332)

Until the mid-1970s, one can find only scattered references to true and fair in the UK accounting literature. For example, the financier Harold Drayton (1962) criticized 'fair' as an ambiguous word and argued that ambiguity did not, or should not, go with facts and figures. In a rather complacent leading article, *The Accountant* (1962, p. 85) replied that:

the words 'true and fair', to whatever they are applied, have a significance far beyond any combination of dictionary meanings. Each time they are used they reflect a professional opinion which is highly valued and, in consequence, never lightly expressed.

In the same year Sir Henry (later Lord) Benson, senior partner of Cooper Bros and a past president of the ICAEW, addressed the Eighth International Congress on Accounting in New York on the subject of auditing in the world economy. In the course of his address he claimed that the meaning attached to true and fair had been:

built up over the years by the standards of presentation specifically required by the Act; established accounting techniques; case law decisions; the natural desire of responsible directors of companies and of auditors to ensure that the facts and figures which are presented to the public properly reflect the position; and, last but not least, by commonsense.

(Benson, 1962, p. 934)

He went on to give what he called 'a broad indication of what is meant by true and fair'. In his view, the term embraced the following:

1 The items in the accounts must be suitably grouped and accurately described so as to indicate their nature.
2 There must be disclosure of the basis used to arrive at the amounts at which fixed assets are stated. Depreciation of fixed assets must be written off year by year on a consistent basis so as to reduce the book value to scrap value at the end of their useful life.
3 Current assets, other than stock-in-trade and work in progress, must be stated at the lower of cost or realisable value.
4 All stock-in-trade and work in progress must be included on a basis which is consistently adopted and is appropriate to the business of the company . . .

5 All liabilities must be included.

6 There must be no 'secret reserves' concealed among the liabilities or created by understating the assets.

7 Trading profits only arise when goods are sold. Profits must not be anticipated, except in exceptional cases of which certain long-term contracts are an example.

8 Exceptional or non-recurring profits or losses must be separately disclosed in the accounts if the amounts are material, and should not normally be included in the trading profits of the year.

9 Full provision must be made for expected losses.

10 Holding companies must publish consolidated accounts or their equivalent . . .

11 The basis of preparing the accounts must be consistently adopted from year to year. Any change of basis, which should only be made with good reason, should be disclosed if the effect on the accounts is material.

12 The specific requirements of the Act must be complied with.

Perhaps this could be summed up as best accounting practice plus the requirements of the Act. There is little indication here of true and fair as an overriding requirement independent of, and superior to, specific rules.

REVIVAL OF UK INTEREST IN TRUE AND FAIR

From the late 1960s onwards, in the UK, interest in discussing true and fair at last started to emerge. There were a number of reasons for this: criticisms of the profession in the financial press in the 1960s; the current cost versus historical cost debate in the 1970s and early 1980s; the Argyll Foods case; the export of the concept to continental Europe via drafts of the Fourth Directive; and (from the 1980s) the growth of creative accounting. Dixon (1969), speaking as President of the English Institute, claimed that truth changed according to the context in which financial statements were presented. Graham (1969), a Scottish CA, foreshadowed the later linking by the UK profession of truth and fairness to accounting standards by wondering whether it would not be 'in the interest of shareholders at large if some of the present freedom regarding presentation was curtailed'. Directors who thought the 'official' basis was misleading could accompany them with an 'unofficial' version which they considered would give 'a truer and fairer view'.

Chastney (1975), published as an Occasional Paper by the Research Committee of the ICAEW, was the first major UK publication on true and fair. This monograph dealt with the history and development of the term and its predecessors in the UK; the meaning of the words 'true', 'fair' and 'true and fair'; legal considerations; accounting considerations; a comparison with other countries; alternatives to true and fair; objectives of financial statements; uniform formats and true and fair. Chastney concluded presciently:

> True and fair now takes on a new lease of life. Its application is to be extended from a few countries connected with the UK to the whole of the European Community. . . . This should not be regarded as a victory for the British profession. Time will tell what the other member states make of 'true and fair'.
>
> (Chastney, 1975, p. 93)

OUTSIDE THE UK

The true and fair requirement was exported to many members of the British Commonwealth (with the notable exception of Canada). It still survives in most of them but was abolished in South Africa in the early 1970s (*South African Chartered Accountant*, 1972).

One of the earliest contributions to the true and fair literature came from New Zealand. Cowan (1965) argued that the British 'true and fair view' and the American 'fair presentation, general acceptance, and consistency' amounted to much the same thing in practice but that both produced unsatisfactory standards of financial reporting because of the lack of a clear definition of the objectives of financial reporting. The later New Zealand literature on true and fair deals mainly with the problem of whether both historical cost accounting (HCA) and current cost accounting (CCA) could be 'true and fair' simultaneously (Harris and Wilson, 1982; Tilly, 1982). Counsel's opinion was obtained by the New Zealand Society of Accountants (*Accountants' Journal*, 1982).

The Australian literature on true and fair is very full and is discussed at length in Chapter 5. Australian writers have paid particular attention to the relationship between true and fair and accounting standards. For reasons discussed in that chapter, Australian standard-setters are now strongly opposed to the true and fair requirement. This attitude is not reflected in the UK literature. Waller (1990), a financial journalist, is an exception in arguing that competitive pressures on both companies and auditors are such that it is now 'time to get rid of true and fair'.

TRUE AND FAIR AND THE CRITICISM
OF HISTORICAL COST

In South Africa and Australia, Eggers (1963) and Horrocks (1967), respectively, linked showing a true and fair view to a departure from historical cost. In the UK, at a time when the issue and acceptance of a CCA standard seemed probable, a number of writers tackled the problem of whether both HCA and CCA could give a true and fair view and what effect this would have on the audit opinion. Jack (1977), a Scottish lawyer, warned that accounts prepared under the historical cost convention would be open to challenge as not providing a true and fair view. Flint (1982, p. 26) thought it clear 'that it would only be in exceptional circumstances that amounts included in accounts determined in accordance with the historical cost accounting rules could on their own, without additions and/or departures' give a true and fair view. Shaw (1979) and Flint (1979) drew attention to the auditor's dilemma: was it appropriate to give a true and fair opinion on two different financial statements (one HCA, the other CCA) in the same annual report? Steele and Haworth (1986) empirically examined the professional consensus on this dilemma. Carslaw (1984) provided examples of how this problem was dealt with in actual audit reports. Lee (1984) and Clarke (1984) discussed the accounting problems, calling for greater flexibility in financial reporting as a route to improved quality. Chambers and Wolnizer (1990, p. 366) argued that a true and fair view is only given if financial statements take account of selling prices, changes in selling prices and changes in the general purchasing power of the unit of account.

THE ARGYLL FOODS CASE AND COUNSELS' OPINION

Jack was one of the few lawyers to comment on true and fair before the Argyll Foods case of 1981 in the UK. A full description and legal analysis of the case is provided in Ashton (1986). The main issue in the case was whether accounts which breached two provisions of the Companies Act 1948 and a statement of standard accounting practice (SSAP 14, on group accounts) gave a true and fair view. The breaches arose as a result of consolidating the balance sheet of a company which at the relevant date was not legally a subsidiary of Argyll Foods (although both companies were managed and effectively controlled by the same people). The audit report stated that the accounting treatment breached the Act and the standard but gave it as the auditors' opinion that, because of the inclusion of information in the Notes, the accounts were not rendered misleading by this non-compliance and that they gave a true and fair view. The case, which was a criminal prosecution, was heard in the Magistrates Court only and was not reported in any of the Law Reports. The magistrates decided that the accounts did not give a true and fair view and therefore contravened the Companies Act. The directors, who were conditionally discharged, did not appeal to a higher court.

Although the case does not constitute a legally binding precedent it has been treated in practice as such because there is a strong presumption that the decision of the magistrates would be followed in a similar case. Directors are unwilling to expose themselves to the possibility of a criminal record and to the costs of appeal. The Department of Trade, which had brought the prosecution, issued a statement which pointed out that the company law amendments of 1981 provide both 'a heightened emphasis on the overriding character of the true and fair requirement' and 'explicit guidance on how it should be fulfilled' and concluded with the somewhat cryptic remark that the Department considered it 'axiomatic that any emphasis on substance over form must not be at the expense of compliance with the law' (Department of Trade, 1982).

The Argyll case was commented on by Bird (1982a, b, 1984), an academic accountant, in both the legal and the accountancy literature. To him the most important point arising from the case was that, where a true and fair view can be given without departing from the specific requirements of the Act (e.g., by the use of pro forma statements), this treatment must be preferred to one which gives a true and fair view by means of a departure from those requirements. In his view, 'Non-compliance is not permitted where compliance together with the provision of additional information would enable a true and fair view to be given' (Bird, 1982a, p. 80). The Accounting Standards Committee obtained the opinions of English and Scottish counsel on the meaning of true and fair (Hoffman and Arden, 1983; Hope, 1984). The opinion of English counsel, with which Scottish counsel agreed, was that *inter alia*:

> the preparation of accounts which give a true and fair view is not merely a matter of compliance with professional standards. ... It is an abstraction or philosophical concept expressed in simple English. ... It is a common feature of such concepts that there is seldom any difficulty in understanding what they mean but frequent controversy over their application to particular facts ... the courts will treat compliance with accepted accounting principles as prima facie evidence that the accounts are true and fair. Equally, deviation from accepted principles will be prima facie evidence that they are not. ... The

meaning of true and fair remains what it was in 1947. It is the content which has changed.

(Hoffman and Arden, 1983)

Grinyer (1984) argued that the Hoffman-Arden opinion threw back on the profession the responsibility for defining true and fair view and called for the Accounting Standards Committee to provide an official definition. This the ASC never did; the Accounting Standards Board has also not attempted to do so. It has, however, stated that the application of the principal qualitative characteristics in its *Statement of Principles*, the law, and appropriate accounting standards should in all normal circumstances result in financial statements 'that convey what is generally understood as a true and fair view'.

The ASB has also obtained an up-dating of the legal opinion on true and fair in the light of the Companies Act 1989. In this, Arden (1993) confirms the previous opinion but strengthens it because the standards and the standard-setters are now recognized in law. She likens accounting standards to customs which are upheld by the courts and thus may properly be regarded as a source of law. The Urgent Issues Task Force (1993) declared that where the true and fair view override is being invoked by a company this should be stated clearly and unambiguously. The UITF sets out how this should be done.

TRUE AND FAIR AND CREATIVE ACCOUNTING

A major problem for standard-setters from the 1980s has been the growth of creative accounting in which the letter of the rules is used to breach the spirit of the rules. This has threatened to turn 'true and fair' into a 'true and fairy tale' (Griffiths, 1986). For example Jackson (1986), an investment analyst, discussed the use of creative accounting techniques by retail companies, and Sugden (1989) draws attention to how creative accounting can extend to the graphs and bar charts included in annual reports. One possible way of tackling the problem of creative accounting (and one that has been recognized by accounting standard-setters: Whitely, 1988) is to use the true and fair concept as a protection against 'creative compliance' with legal rules:

> far from providing too flexible a framework for the exercise of directors' discretion, this philosophy denies to directors the possibility of using the protection of a narrow legalistic compliance with detailed prescriptive requirements to avoid embarrassing disclosures of necessary information which the prescription has failed to procure.
>
> (Flint, 1982, p. 5)

Both Flint (1982, p. 32) and Woolf (1986, p. 119) see auditors as the monitors and guardians against abuse. Their ability to use the true and fair requirement in this way is discussed by Tweedie (1988, pp. 2–3), who distinguishes between true and fair in its 'progressive' form as an instrument for the replacement of 'antiquated laws' and 'outdated accounting standards' and its 'regressive' form where audit firms are held back because they may be at commercial disadvantage if they take a stand against a practice accepted by many of their competitors and hence, it is argued, 'part of the practices encompassed by the true and fair view'.

Tweedie clearly prefers the progressive form. But who then has the right to break the rules? In Australia (see Chapter 5) it is directors who have successfully claimed this privilege, to the extent that Australian standard-setters have tried to abolish the true and fair requirement. In the UK, the accounting standard-setters have claimed the right and have, as a consequence, found themselves at loggerheads with the legal profession on issues concerning off-balance sheet financing and window-dressing. An ICAEW Technical Release (TR 603, Feb. 1986) argued that giving a true and fair view required the pre-eminence of economic substance over legal form. This accountants' view was promptly described in a Law Society memorandum as 'dangerous and undesirable' and 'contrary to law'.

In the discussion between accountants and lawyers which ensued, the issue of territorial claims was explicitly recognized. 'Ultimately' wrote Tweedie and Kellas (1987, p. 93), 'what is at stake is the custodianship of the concept of the true and fair view', which, quoting Hoffman and Arden's (1983) legal opinion in support, they argued was what the accountancy profession says it is – 'unless the profession takes collective leave of its senses and moves too far from commercial acceptability'. They distinguished their position from that of the Law Society as follows: 'The Law Society appears to be arguing that generally the legal form should be shown in the financial statements; fairness (i.e., economic substance) can be covered by additional disclosure in the notes: we are arguing for the converse' (Tweedie and Kellas, 1987, p. 93). They concluded that the true and fair concept 'should be used not as an excuse for not obeying the rules but as a safeguard against loopholes being sought in the rules' (ibid., p. 95).

The discussion continued with a lawyer, Ardwinckle (1987), arguing that the Companies Act 1981 (as consolidated in the 1985 Act) had made the true and fair requirement more legalistic and less flexible. Detailed requirements of the Act could only be departed from if additional information failed to give a true and fair view. He pointed out that one could not always be confident as to what constituted economic substance: it may look quite different to, say, a creditor and an investment analyst (Ardwinckle, 1987, p. 19). Wild (1987) called for better cooperation between accountants and lawyers so as not to 'leave the accounts easy prey to those with no real interest in the law' (Wild, 1987, p. 21).

Tweedie and Kellas (1988), in their reply to Ardwinckle, argued that what is a true and fair view was a question to be determined by the accountancy profession, not by legal analysis. They disagreed with Ardwinckle's contention that the Companies Act allowed departure only after extra information. True and fair, they argued, was 'an ambulatory concept – it moves on with changing practice, it consists of the corpus of practices acceptable at that time to the profession, business and the government.' This assumes that directors will not over-emphasize 'true' as distinct from 'fair' and that auditors are willing and able to monitor the concept. Nobes and Parker's empirical findings (1991; see Chapter 2) cast some doubt on the former; Tweedie (1988) draws attention to the difficulties that auditors face in a competitive audit market.

Demirag and Macve (1986a, b) discuss the problem of the true and fair override in relation to the treatment of long-term contract work in progress. Pawson (1987) sets out the Accounting Standards Committee's ingenious way of reclassifying asset items in order to avoid use of the override.

According to Flint, the true and fair concept also:

> provides protection to users from political and other bias, from deficiency or inadequacy in the rules, and from any other shortcomings of prescription. In Great Britain, practice in corporate financial reporting has, in the past, developed ahead of legal prescription; the reporting standard of 'a true and fair view' enables it to continue to do so.
>
> (Flint, 1984, p. 109)

EMPIRICAL RESEARCH

The true and fair literature is not notable for an emphasis on empirical research. Donleavy (1990) tested students' grasp of truth and fairness before and after encountering funds statements. Nobes and Parker (1991; see Chapter 2) and Parker and Nobes (1991; see Chapter 3) surveyed the ways in which UK financial directors and auditors, respectively, operationalized the requirement to give, and report on, a true and fair view. Higson and Blake (1993, pp. 111–14) also surveyed auditors' views with results that appear to differ from those of Parker and Nobes (perhaps because they asked different questions).

Readers of the literature on true and fair can be forgiven for believing that the concept was invented for the benefit of lawyers and accountants. Balfour (1984, p. 319) wonders what the lay person's conception of a true and fair view is. This is an empirical question which has been researched in part by Houghton (1987) who looked at the differences between Australian accountants' and shareholders' perceptions of the meaning of true and fair. He reported significant differences between the responses of the two groups and, moreover, that the accountants could not accurately perceive the shareholders' meaning.

TRUE AND FAIR AND THE EC

Not surprisingly, most discussion of true and fair as applicable in Continental Europe since the implementation of the Fourth Directive has been in languages other than English. There is already a large literature in French and German. A small part of this literature is, however, in English. Lasok and Grace, respectively a lawyer and an accountant, writing in a legal journal, argue that true and fair 'has effectively ceased to designate a concept of English law and now refers to a concept of European Community law' (Lasok and Grace, 1988, p. 236). McGee, an academic lawyer, argues that to regard the true and fair requirement as a protection against the detailed rules of the EC Directives is misplaced because it confuses the intention of the UK with the legal effect of what has been done, which has been 'to give the requirement an even greater legal status than it previously had' (McGee, 1991, p. 877). Parker (1989) points out that the British (as 'active exporters') were keener to export the true and fair concept than the Continental Europeans (as 'passive importers') were to import it. Unlike the export of true and fair to Australasia, the words needed to be translated. The problems of doing this are discussed by Rutherford (1983) and by Nobes (1993; see chapter 4). Looking at the problem from the other direction, Zeff (1990) discusses the translation of the Dutch expression '*geeft een getrouw beeld*' (see Appendix I).

Pham (1984) discusses the problems that French accountants have had in interpreting true and fair, distinguishing between what he calls the 'extremists' (divided into the 'ultra-conservatives' for whom true and fair is merely a change in terminology, and the 'ultra-liberals' who would like to see true and fair as a means of escaping from restrictive rules) and the 'moderates' (divided into those who wish to see true and fair as a rule for interpreting the information conveyed in financial statements, and those who would use true and fair in the preparation of the statements).

Busse von Colbe (1984) and Ordelheide (1993) discuss true and fair from a German perspective. Busse von Colbe (1984, p. 122) points out that the true and fair view concept is 'alien to German accounting rules'. He finds it difficult to imagine 'a case which forced [German] companies to deviate from the detailed regulations' (ibid., p. 124). Ordelheide (1993) reports a number of German interpretations of the relationship between true and fair and the requirement to comply with *Grundsätze ordnungsmässiger Buchführung* (GoB). The 'separation thesis' (*Abkopplungsthese*) states that, where true and fair accounting is not equivalent to accounting according to GoB, additional information in the notes is sufficient in order to establish a true and fair view. Other German authors agree that it is not acceptable to use in the balance sheet and profit and loss account an accounting method which provides a true and fair view but contradicts the GoB but argue further that, if there are several methods acceptable under GoB but not all provide a true and fair view, then GoB is thereby restricted. Zeff *et al.* (1992) discuss true and fair from a Dutch perspective.

Alexander, Burlaud, Ordelheide and Van Hulle, in a special section of the *European Accounting Review* (May 1993) consider the EC dimensions of true and fair. Alexander points out that Article 2 of the Fourth Directive dealing with true and fair has been implemented in substantially different ways in the UK, France and Germany and concludes that a 'common Europe-wide view of TFV implies a common and homogeneous culture' (Alexander 1993, p. 75) which he clearly regards as neither desirable nor likely to come into being. Ordelheide (1993, p. 81) points out, however, that from a legal point of view the 'true and fair principle is an autonomous European norm' and that in the event of a European conflict its content would be decided not by a national court but by the European Court. This point is also stressed by Van Hulle, who goes on to argue that: 'it is therefore perfectly possible that annual accounts which are regarded as true and fair in one Member State would not be interpreted as such in another Member State' (Van Hulle, 1993, pp. 99–100).

It is Ordelheide's view that exporting true and fair to Continental Europe may have unintended consequences for the British accountancy profession. He argues that the 'gateway of Art. 2 (5) seems too narrow for all deviations of British accounting from the accounting principles of the Fourth Directive' (Ordelheide, 1993, pp. 83–4). Nobes (1993; see Chapter 4) comments on these papers and suggests a continuum of importance of the true and fair requirement in different EC countries. Burlaud (1993, pp. 94, 98) sees true and fair as a guide for standard-setters rather than for enterprises.

TRUE AND FAIR AND LIFE ASSURANCE

A small sub-set of the true and fair literature (Smart, 1985; Whewell, 1990; Brady and Healy, 1991; Mynors, 1992) deals with the accounts of life assurance companies where there is a clash between true and fair accounts and the statutory accounts required by the Department of Trade which are based on solvency on a break-up basis, using very conservative assumptions. Movement towards the former has been hastened by the implementation of the EC directive on insurers' accounts, the problems of incorporating a life assurance company into a wider group, and last, but not least, the search for deterrents to hostile takeover bids.

WHAT DOES TRUE AND FAIR 'MEAN'?

Fowle (1992, p. 29), a practitioner, argues that 'even 20 years ago [the early 1970s] . . . a leading auditor would not have had any difficulty in saying what a true and fair view meant. "True" was intended to convey the essence of "correct", without pedantic accuracy, while "fair" recognised that a true statement may nevertheless give a misleading view.' He concludes that 'a true and fair view' is 'a concept no more capable of facile definition than its legal equivalent of equity, and just as vital to financial reporting as the concept of equity is to law'.

Academic writers have found it more difficult to establish the 'meaning' of true and fair. They have even referred to it as a 'will-o'-the wisp' (Lee, 1982; Forster, 1983). Lee (1982, p. 16) suggests that 'accountants have collectively and subconsciously agreed that "truth and fairness" is something that requires no interpretation; that its meaning is known to every producer, auditor and user of external financial statements without formal announcement'. It has been argued that this lack of definition is in fact a strength of the concept. Popoff (1983, p. 52) claims that the very problems involved in its interpretation in practical situations provide a stimulus for a continuing critical examination of accounting methods and procedures and of the quality and relevance of the statements produced therefrom. Chambers and Wolnizer (1990, p. 358) are unusual in arguing that despite the phrase *'a* true and fair view' in the legislation there can be only one true and fair view of a company at any point in time.

Although Chastney (1975, p. 48) did not provide a definition he quoted approvingly G.A. Lee's statement that:

> It is generally understood to mean a presentation of accounts, drawn up according to accepted accounting principles, using accurate figures as far as possible, and reasonable estimates otherwise; and arranging

them so as to show, within the limits of current accounting practice, as objective a picture as possible, free from wilful bias, manipulation, or concealment of material facts.

> (G.A. Lee, *Modern Financial Accounting*, Nelson, 1973, p. 31)

This definition can be compared with T.A. Lee's:

> True means that the accounting information contained in the financial statements has been quantified and communicated in such a way as to correspond to the economic events, activities and transactions it is intended to describe.... Fair means that the accounting information has been measured and disclosed in a manner which is objective and without prejudice to any particular sectional interests in the company.
>
> (Lee, 1986, p. 51)

Higson and Blake identify 'four separate distinct and not totally complementary' meanings:

1 As a relaxation of previous accounting rules, acknowledging that various areas of judgment and estimation arise in the preparation of financial statements;
2 as a strengthening of previous accounting rules, effectively moving towards a 'substance over form' approach;
3 as an assertion that the financial statements should be free from bias; and
4 as a basis for the assertion of the authority of the technical pronouncements emerging from the accounting profession.

> ((Higson and Blake, 1993, p. 108)

Rutherford (1985, p. 489) points out that G.A. Lee's approach could be described as 'bottom up'; in which case T.A. Lee's could be described as 'top down'. Rutherford argues that either the true and fair concept should be abandoned or it should be 'explained' (rather than precisely defined) as compliance with generally accepted accounting principles. A top-down approach implies that the words 'true and fair' should be given their ordinary and natural lay usage rather than be regarded as technical accounting terms (Wolnizer, 1985).

Bottom-up approaches to true and fair have been put forward by a number of writers. As early as 1971 Edey argued that 'true and fair' was 'a term of art' – a technical term that meant nothing more than that all the specific legal requirements and usual accounting conventions had been followed: a view consistent with Benson's (1962) broad definition quoted above but challenged by Chambers and Wolnizer

(1990, p. 359). Macve and Jackson (1991, p. 59) also regard true and fair as a 'legal term of art, reflecting in the main what users may reasonably expect to find in a set of accounts'. In their view the general acceptance of an accounting procedure, e.g. marking to market, is a powerful argument for regarding it as true and fair.

Chopping and Skerratt (1993, p. 43) see the concept of true and fair as being implemented by a combination of current rules, current accepted practice and amendments to those rules and practices. Walton (1991) also implicitly argues from a bottom-up viewpoint, placing an emphasis on what is 'signified', which is constantly shifting, rather than on the 'signifier' (the words 'true and fair'). For him true and fair merely refers to a set of generally accepted accounting principles (GAAP) which is 'simply a collection of solutions to past problems, arising in a particular economic community, collected together over the years and not relating to any particular underlying principle' (Walton, 1993, p. 52). Taking the bottom-up approach to the extreme, the actual words, including those in legal regulations, 'do not matter, since these are merely signifiers, and what is important is the signified' (ibid., p. 53). This is a view which lawyers find difficult to accept. Lasok and Grace (1989, p. 16), for example, argue that 'just because certain specific rules of accounting practice are generally accepted by the accounting profession does not mean that they satisfy the standard required by the Companies Act and the Fourth Directive'. McGee (1991, p. 887) also insists that the true and fair test 'is a legal one, and cannot be a matter purely for accountants, however much they might wish otherwise'. He admits, however, to 'the evident lack of any clear legally based explanation of what true and fair means'.

Supporters of the top-down approach argue that true and fair is, or should be, a 'transcendent' concept, i.e. one that is, or should be, above and independent of detailed accounting practice. Flint is a leading proponent of this view, arguing that 'a detailed prescriptive approach must always be to some extent inadequate, invariably out of date as legislation lags behind the need for change, and inappropriate as situations arise which have not been foreseen and provided for' (Flint, 1982, p. 4). A true and fair view is not susceptible to 'being defined conclusively and completely by a set of prescriptive rules setting out in detail how accounts should be prepared, what information should be disclosed, what basis of valuation should be used' (Flint, 1984, p. 101). In the words of Woolf (1986, p. 119), 'definitions invariably invite attempts to satisfy their letter while deliberately ignoring their spirit, thereby avoiding their main purpose'.

Flint (1982, p. 2) views true and fair as a 'philosophical concept' and it has in fact attracted the attention of philosophers. Harris (1987), unlike most accountants and lawyers, concentrates on the needs of users, suggesting that preparers and auditors should approach financial statements as if they had an equal chance of being a user or a preparer. Lyas (1992, pp. 162–3) points out that 'true' and 'fair' are 'terms with a philosophical baggage'.

Harris's approach from philosophy receives some support from Tweedie (1983, p. 449):

> While the detailed requirements necessary to show a true and fair view will continually evolve as social attitudes and technical skills change, the basic question to be posed by both director and auditor will remain 'if I were on "the outside" and did not have the detailed knowledge of the company's trading performance and ultimate financial position that I have as I look at these accounts, would I be able to obtain a *clear and unambiguous* picture of that reality from these accounts?'
>
> (italics in original)

It is obviously easier to operationalize the bottom-up approach than the top-down approach. This does not seem to worry Stewart (1988, p. 121) who finds the foundation of true and fair 'in natural law and justice'. Most supporters of the top-down approach, however, assume that true and fair accounts will comply with statutory requirements and accounting standards. The difference from the bottom-up approach is that, 'an understanding of the true and fair view is necessary *before* devising statutory requirements, accounting principles or accounting standards designed to contribute to its achievement. These are the means to the end and not the end itself' (Flint, 1978, p. 488, italics added).

Tweedie sees statutory prescription as a first stage, to be followed by stepping back and considering the impression given by the financial statements: 'Truth alone is not enough – truth can still give a misleading impression if presented in an appropriate context' (Tweedie, 1983, p. 425).

The dichotomy between the approaches is considered in Gwilliam and Russell's (1991) discussion of whether Polly Peck's 1989 accounts gave a true and fair view. They conclude that the present compromise in practice between the two approaches is unsatisfactory. Either standards must be made more prescriptive (SSAP 20 on foreign currency translation being insufficiently so in the Polly Peck case) or there must be 'enhanced reliance on the depiction of economic reality' (Gwilliam and Russell, 1991, p. 35). But, they argue, the latter approach cannot succeed unless 'the client service mentality which currently pervades [the UK auditing profession] is replaced by a greater emphasis on the auditor as an independent monitor'.

There has been some discussion whether the words 'true' and 'fair' should be considered separately or as a hendiadys (i.e. the expression of a complex idea by two words connected by 'and') (Forster, 1983). Lee (1982, p. 18) argues for the former, and Dyer (1974) has provided a detailed analysis of the 'meaning of "true" in "true and fair".' For Davison (1983, p. 3) however, 'true and fair view is . . . a hyphenated phrase which loses its essential meaning if the words are considered separately. Like a bicycle, it has two wheels, true and fair. Take one away and the vehicle falls over.'

Williams (1985, pp. 25–6) and Rutherford (1989, pp. 135–6) draw attention to the extension in the UK of the true and fair concept beyond company financial statements to, according to Williams, no less than seventy-five other Acts of Parliament. Exported to Continental Europe and extended beyond company law, the true and fair concept looks likely to feature in the world's accounting literature in English and in other languages for many years to come.

NOTE

1 All references in this chapter are to works in the bibliography.

2 'True and Fair'

A Survey of UK Financial Directors[1]

ABSTRACT

The legal and philosophical meanings of 'true and fair' have been discussed elsewhere. This paper is the first published empirical survey of what directors say they *do* to ensure that financial statements are true and fair. A questionnaire survey (with a high response rate) of large British companies allows the conclusions that most directors take no specific actions, that they rely heavily on auditors, and that they equate 'true' and 'fair'. Some directors seem to misunderstand their duties. Subsidiaries take a more mechanical view of compliance.

INTRODUCTION

This paper reports the results of a survey of how large UK companies, according to replies received to a questionnaire addressed to their finance directors, apply in practice the concept of a 'true and fair view' to their organizations' financial statements.

The concept of a true and fair view is central to accounting in the UK and is regarded by British accountants as one of its fundamental characteristics. Since 1947 it has been the overriding requirement of company law. The requirements of the Acts of 1948 (s. 149) and 1985 (s. 228, which re-enacts the relevant section of the 1981 Act) are set out in Appendix 2.1. The concept has been exported to a number of Commonwealth countries (notably Australia and New Zealand) and more recently, through the Fourth Directive on company accounts, to the member states of the European Communities (Parker, 1989).

The true and fair concept has never received an authoritative definition from a judge or an accountancy body but, if pressed to state what they understand by it, many UK practising accountants might accept Rutteman's (1984, p. 8) statement that it comprises both 'fairness of presentation' (i.e. lack of bias as between the different users of financial information) and the 'recognition of economic substance rather than mere legal form'. Both fairness of presentation and substance over form have received added importance in recent years with the rise of 'creative accounting' (as spelled out in Griffiths, 1986), i.e. the use of accounting to mislead rather than to help the intended user of financial statements. Leading UK practitioners have recommended the use of the true and fair concept to combat the perceived evils of such creative devices as off balance sheet financing (Tweedie and Kellas, 1987). On the other hand, one of our respondents did not see true and fair as inconsistent with creative accounting and income smoothing:

> Provided that the ideas in [Griffiths'] book and other ideas are used sensibly with a view to trending long-term profits, all is well. There is nothing magical about a twelve-month period. What is important is that statutory accounts reflect long-term profits, not short-term fluctuations. Indeed to present short-term results as *the* results does not give a true and fair view in its wider sense.

The substance-over-form approach has, however, been attacked by the Law Society (1986), commenting on a Technical Release issued by the Institute of Chartered Accountants in England and Wales, as 'subjective', 'vague', 'dangerous', 'undesirable' and 'contrary to law'.

In these circumstances we see a clear need to discover how the true and fair concept operates in practice. In particular we ask financial directors in our survey what their companies do, *in addition* to complying with company law and accounting standards, to ensure that their financial statements give a true and fair view. It might be suggested that such a question is unanswerable (and therefore ought not to be asked) on two possible grounds: *either* that true and fair is (or should be) a 'transcendent' concept, i.e. it is above and independent of detailed accounting practice and thus cannot (or should not) be tied down to doing anything separately identifiable; *or* that giving a true and fair view does not (or should not) mean anything more than complying with company legislation and accounting standards. As can be observed, both objections can be expressed either normatively or positively.

Normatively, there seem to be two views. According to the first set of arguments, true and fair is regarded as incapable of definition. To Flint (1982, p. 2) true and fair is a philosophical concept and the fact that it is not susceptible to definition by a comprehensive set of detailed rules is its 'most fundamental and characteristic feature'. What is perceived to be true and fair is, Flint argues, 'ultimately a matter of ethics or morality' (ibid., p. 30). This seems implicitly to assume that the preparers, auditors *and the users* of financial statements all share a common understanding of the purposes of financial reporting, and that, in some indefinable way, choices between alternative accounting procedures are made by managers, verified by auditors and accepted by shareholders on the basis of a consensus as to what is fair.

It is possible that this view is held by some British finance directors (a large majority of whom are qualified accountants). Indeed, one of the respondents to our questionnaire wrote to us as follows:

> The questionnaire appears to be based upon the assumption that 'true and fair' is some sort of magic formula which is kept locked in a box and which has to be taken out in specific circumstances, first to refresh the memory and then to be applied to the situation in hand. It is rather like asking an advanced motorist how often he has to drive on the left hand side of the road and apply the highway code. The true and fair concept is something which is ingrained in accountants. I am fairly sure that in all our discussions with the auditors, and we have many, the term 'true and fair' has never once been used. It is a concept that we all hold in common and is not a matter for discussion.

It is certainly difficult to discover in auditing textbooks or audit manuals a set of procedures for testing whether accounts give a true and fair view. A set of procedures of a Big Eight firm which does do so is reproduced in Hopkins (1984, pp. 48–9). An analysis of this shows that the only items which do not overlap with compliance with the *specific* provisions of the Companies Act and accounting standards are:

1 Presentation which is not misleading, ambiguous or obscure.
2 Substance over form.

These are essentially the same points made by Rutteman (1984) and quoted above.

At the other extreme it could be argued that 'true and fair' should simply mean detailed compliance with a set of 'generally accepted accounting principles' contained (in the context of UK methods of accounting regulation) in company law and statements of standard accounting practice. This may well be the situation in the USA where financial statements are stated to 'present fairly' financial position and results 'in conformity with generally accepted principles'. (Nevertheless, a proposal in 1980 by the Auditing Standards Board of the American Institute of Certified Public Accountants that the word 'fairly' be deleted provoked much debate and disagreement and was eventually withdrawn: Carmichael and Winters, 1982, p. 18.) However, UK legislation specifically requires companies to depart from the accounting rules in the Companies Act where this is necessary to give a true and fair view, and it is counsel's opinion (Hoffman and Arden, 1983) that compliance with accounting standards is only prima facie evidence that a true and fair view has been given, suggesting that a true and fair view involves, on occasion, something more than mere compliance with the rules currently in existence.

Given that these two views are normative, we cannot usefully attempt to prove their validity by argument. However, they suggest that it is legitimate to ask, as we do in our survey, what financial directors do, in addition to complying with the detailed rules of company legislation and accounting standards, to ensure that the financial statements that they publish give, as the law requires, a true and fair view. Of course, questionnaire surveys of necessity report what the respondents say that they do, which may not be what they actually do. Given the clear indications of the law we would expect the bias, if there is one, to be towards overstating rather than understating the procedures taken to ensure truth and fairness.

It is not easy, a priori, to suggest how a director can know what is a true and fair view. Little help has been provided by the lawyers. As Williams (1985, p. 27) points out, true and fair is a legal concept on which there is 'a dearth of comment by the judges and by academic commentators'. The few reported cases provide little guidance: 'it is a law that only one person [Argyll Foods] has apparently ever been prosecuted for breaking, and one that courts do not enforce through civil actions' (ibid., p. 29).

If true and fair is a philosophic (although not necessarily a trans-cendent) concept, one might look for help to the philosophers. So far as we are aware, only one philosopher has discussed the concept. Harris (1987) makes use of Rawls' (1972) notion of a 'veil of ignorance' to provide a possible way of ensuring that, in the preparation of company financial statements, equal regard is paid to interests of all users. Harris's suggestion is that the preparers and auditors should ask themselves the following question. If one had an equal chance of being either a producer of financial statements or a user of them, what sort of requirements would one prefer? This is related to the procedure to ensure that two people will divide a cake fairly: one of them cuts the cake into two parts and the other then chooses his part. There is an economic literature on fairness and 'superfairness' (Baumol, 1986), but no attempt has been made to apply this to financial reporting. Harris (1987) also suggests the adoption of the 'Mischief Rule', i.e. the inter-pretation of the concept in accord with what it is meant to accomplish. This would mean that compliance with the rules would not be regarded as sufficient if the financial statements still gave a misleading impression.

We turn now to a positive theory approach to true and fair. What incentives are there for the managers of different types of companies to signal to the shareholders and other users of their published financial statements that those statements give a true and fair view? Whilst all companies are likely to be concerned to comply with the law, it is possible that different types of companies may have incentives to interpret compliance differently. A study of the literature suggests that both the composition of shareholders and size of company may be relevant in this connection.

The agency-theory literature stresses the relevance to the actions of managers not just of the capital structure of companies but also of the composition of the shareholdings (Jensen and Meckling, 1976, pp. 327, 343; and Dhaliwal, Salmon and Smith, 1982). Two extremes are: listed parent companies with widely dispersed shareholdings and subsidiary companies with only one major shareholder. The former's financial statements will be closely monitored by shareholders and investment analysts. The latter's financial statements will create no such general interest, especially if the major shareholder is located overseas in a country without a true and fair view requirement. The major shareholder will in any case have full access to any information that it requires. If the parent is the only user of the financial statements there are no incentives for such subsidiaries to do more than comply with the specific provisions of the Act and accounting standards. Providing additional information or departing from the specific regulations would not serve the needs of the user.

The size hypothesis suggests that the 'political costs' of being perceived not to give a true and fair view will be greatest for the very largest companies, i.e. those whose activities are of such economic and social significance that their financial statements are likely to be closely monitored not only by shareholders and investment analysts (if they are listed companies) but also by politicians and the press. How might such a perception of not giving a true and fair view arise? The most obvious means is through a qualified audit report. However, even with an audit report which does suggest that the accounts are true and fair, there could be court cases or press speculation to challenge this. Therefore, for the type of companies discussed in this paragraph, the directors are likely to wish to signal strongly that they take all necessary actions, including getting a clean audit report and giving additional information, to ensure that their accounts are seen to give a true and fair view. It is uncertain a priori, however, whether they perceive *departures* from the specific rules of the Act and accounting standards as a favourable signal (showing a willingness to give a true and fair view at all costs) or as an unfavourable signal (drawing unnecessary attention to the company's problems).

Hypotheses such as these, unlike those relating to choices of particular accounting methods and their effect on reported income (see, for example, Zmijewski and Hagerman, 1981), are difficult to test other than by questionnaire or by interview. This is not a disadvantage, however, since in a signalling context what directors say they do is just as important as what they actually do. Thus, although the empirical literature on management's choice of accounting methods makes no reference to fairness, it is consistent with that literature (e.g. Ball and Foster, 1982) to hypothesize that the managers of certain types of companies (1. parent companies, 2. large companies) will have more incentive than those of other types (1. subsidiary companies, 2. small companies) to take actions to ensure that their published statements can be seen to give a true and fair view. As part of this paper, we address the parent/subsidiary issue, leaving the size hypothesis for a later study.

COMPANIES SURVEYED

The survey reported in this paper was limited to the top 900 companies listed in *The Times 1000, 1985/86*. This is a list of industrial companies and excludes financial institutions (banks, insurance companies, building societies, investment trusts, unit trusts etc.) and property companies. Many of these non-industrial companies are subject to separate and complex legislation relating to published financial information. *The Times 1000* is not, however, confined to listed companies and includes subsidiaries (mainly of non-UK companies) as well as parent companies. It also includes state-owned companies (e.g. British Rail). Whilst most of these companies are not subject to the Companies Act they usually either have a true and fair requirement in their own Acts or voluntarily accept that requirement. A number of companies in the list have either recently been privatized or were at the date of the survey in the process of being privatized.

As explained below, 463 companies responded to our questionnaire. They can be classified as follows:

parents	334
subsidiaries	112
other (i.e. publicly owned)	17
	463

HYPOTHESES

It is a plausible hypothesis that the finance directors of subsidiaries (given the great increases in recent years in the quantity and complexity of these rules and the absence of a widely dispersed shareholding) take no specific actions, beyond complying with the Act and SSAPs, to ensure that the annual accounts give a true and fair view, but rely instead upon the auditors to ensure that this requirement is complied with. This hypothesis is less plausible for parents and state-owned companies.

Since 1981, UK directors have been specifically required in certain circumstances to provide additional information or to depart from the specific provisions of the Companies Act or to do both (now s.228, Companies Act 1985; see Appendix 2.1). Here again it seems plausible to argue that there no incentives for subsidiaries to take these actions, but some incentives for parents and others.

Accounting writers (e.g. Chastney, 1975) have sometimes discussed the distinction between 'true' and 'fair', suggesting that what is true is not necessarily fair. Cowan (1965) gives the amusing analogy of the mutually antagonistic sober captain and drunken mate of a tramp steamer who wrote in the ship's log on consecutive days: 'The mate was drunk today', and 'The captain was sober today'. Both statements were true but not necessarily fair. On the other hand, those continental European countries which have translated 'true and fair view' into their own language have generally chosen one word (e.g. *fidèle* in French, *fiel* in Spanish, *getrouw* in Dutch) to represent 'true and fair' (Rutherford, 1983; and Parker, 1989). Our hypothesis is that most directors do not distinguish between what is true and what is fair.

The Companies Act requires directors to furnish annual accounts that give a true and fair view (s.228) and auditors to state whether in their opinion such a view is given (s.236). There is no requirement, however (as there is, for example, in the Australian Companies Act and Codes) for directors to make a formal statement in the annual report that the annual accounts give a true and fair view. In such circumstances one might expect that the auditors would require from a company each year a statement that, in the directors' opinion, the accounts give a true and fair view. We hypothesise that such is usually the case.

Expressed in testable form, our hypotheses are as follows:

H_1: Over 50 per cent of finance directors take no specific actions to ensure that the annual accounts give a true and fair view.

H_2: Over 50 per cent of the directors rely on auditors to ensure that law, standards and 'true and fair view' are obeyed.

H_3:   Over 50 per cent of the directors do not distinguish between 'true' and 'fair'.

H_4:   Over 50 per cent of the directors are unclear about their responsibility to provide, in certain circumstances, additional information or to depart from the specific requirements of the Act.

H_5:   Companies that have parents (overseas or domestic) are more likely to rely on auditors and to take a mechanical view of compliance with rules.

H_6:   Over 50 per cent of auditors require companies to provide each year a statement that, in the directors' opinion, the accounts give a true and fair view.

SURVEY RESULTS

A pilot questionnaire concerning directors' actions (rather than their opinions) was sent in early 1986 to finance directors of the smallest 100 companies in *The Times 1000*. After small amendments, the questionnaire was sent in mid-1986 to the top 900 companies, with a follow-up letter to non-respondents in late 1986. The usable response rate was 51 per cent (i.e. 463 companies),[1] with no detectable non-response bias (see section on Limitations). Internal consistency was reasonably high, as checked by some cross-tabulations.[2] The text of the questionnaire is given in Appendix 2.2.

The most interesting results[3] are presented in Tables 2.1 to 2.8. In most cases separate data are shown for those companies (24 per cent of our respondents) that are subsidiaries. In Table 2.1, percentages are given of companies using particular techniques to ensure compliance with the Act. It may be seen that the majority of companies use both checklists and audit advice. For compliance with standards, there is less

Table 2.1 Techniques of compliance with the Companies Act

	Respondents	Used Checklists		Used Auditors		Used Reference Books	
		No.	%	No.	%	No.	%
Parents	328	182	55	252	77	46	14
Subsidiaries	112	49	44	93	83	14	13
All Respondents	440	231	52	345	79	60	13

Note: Many companies use more than one technique.

use of such techniques (presumably because the adverse consequences of non-compliance are also less) though reference to auditors remains high (see Table 2.2).

The *degree* to which directors report reliance on auditors is shown in Tables 2.3 and 2.4. It may be seen that a minority of directors rely solely on auditors for compliance with law, standards or true and fair. For our sample, full reliance is more common among subsidiaries, particularly for standards and law. For both types of company and requirement, the large majority of companies rely on auditors to some extent. Reliance on auditors seems reasonable since, as discussed

Table 2.2 Techniques of compliance with accounting standards

	Respondents	Used Checklists		Used Auditors		Used Reference Books	
		No.	%	No.	%	No.	%
Parents	323	106	33	218	67	35	11
Subsidiaries	110	30	27	88	80	11	10
All Respondents	433	136	31	306	70	46	10

Note: Many companies use more than one technique.

Table 2.3 Reliance on auditors (by parents) to ensure compliance

	Companies Act		Standards		True and Fair		True=Fair*
	No.	%	No.	%	No.	%	%
Full	29	8	23	7	22	7	94
Partial	257	78	256	78	235	72	83
None	42	13	49	15	70	21	77
All Respondents	328	99	328	100	327	100	

Note: *This column is for reference. It shows the percentage of all respondent companies (for each degree of reliance) whose directors believe that 'true' equals 'fair'.

Table 2.4 Reliance on auditors (by subsidiaries) to ensure compliance

	Companies Act		Standards		True and Fair	
	No.	%	No.	%	No.	%
Full	24	21	17	15	11	10
Partial	80	71	86	77	76	68
None	8	7	9	8	25	22
All Respondents	112	99	112	100	112	100

earlier, a qualified audit report is the main method of its becoming clear that directors have broken details of the law or not given a true and fair view. However, it is interesting that parents report less reliance on auditors than subsidiaries do. This suggests that some directors (particularly those of large independent companies) do feel a responsibility to give (or a political need to be seen to give) a true and fair view, beyond merely satisfying the auditors on this point.

Table 2.5 reports on four points relating to true and fair. Once directors are satisfied that the accounts comply with standards and the details of the law, do they do anything else to ensure that there is a true and fair view? It seems that only a minority do (48 per cent of parents, 34 per cent of subsidiaries). This is a major finding, suggesting that, for most companies, giving a 'true and fair view' means no more than complying with the Companies Act and accounting standards. We asked respondents to specify what additional specific steps they took. The replies are difficult to categorize but most referred to a review (either of the financial statements in general or of specific items) by the directors, the audit committee or even by outsiders. A few stressed the importance of presentation and of substance over form. Some of the replies were rather vague and, if anything, our survey results over-estimate the proportion of companies which take additional steps. Related to this is the finding, in the second column of Table 2.5, that for over 80 per cent of companies 'true' equals 'fair'. This seems to fit with a perception that obeying the rules is enough. Further, the last column of Table 2.3 suggests that the more the reliance on auditors, the greater the belief that 'true' and 'fair' are synonymous.

Table 2.5 also shows that a minority of companies (and particularly few subsidiaries) have disclosed extra information in order to ensure truth and fairness. In addition a majority of boards (particularly of subsidiaries) were required to confirm to the auditors that the accounts were thought to be true and fair. There seems to be some inconsistency here,

Table 2.5 True and fair

	Respondents	Additional Steps Taken		Belief that True=Fair		Disclosure of Additional Information		Directors Provide Statement	
		No.	%	No.	%	No.	%	No.	%
Parents	320	153	48	264	81	115	35	187	58
Subsidiaries	111	37	34	97	88	19	17	94	85
All Respondents	431	190	43	361	83	134	32	281	65

in that some boards must be sending confirmations to the auditors even though they rely heavily on the auditors and have taken no specific steps to ensure truth and fairness.

Tables 2.6 and 2.7 show the percentages of companies that would be willing to depart, and those that have departed, from standards or the details of the law in order to give a true and fair view. The most remarkable finding is that only 71 per cent of parents and 55 per cent of subsidiaries would be prepared to depart from a detailed requirement of the Act. This is despite the Act's insistence on such departures. It seems unlikely that this can be explained in most cases by the directors not imagining that relevant special circumstances for departure could arise, because the question (No. 9a) is fairly clear, in the subjunctive, and contrasted to an actual departure. As shown in Tables 2.6 and 2.7, substantial minorities have departed from standards and details of the law. In all cases, subsidiaries are more hesitant. A number of companies informed us that they departed from the specific requirements of the Act in order to show a true and fair view of the valuation of long-term contract work in progress. (This departure reflects the view that the inclusion of attributable profit as required by SSAP 9 may have been contrary to the Companies Act 1985, Schedule 4, paragraph 22.)

Table 2.6 Departures from details of law to ensure true and fair

	Respondents	Willing to		Departed		Auditors Agreed*	
		No.	%	No.	%	No.	%
Parents	304	251	71	56	17	53	91
Subsidiaries	103	57	55	5	4	4	80
All Respondents	407	308	66	61	14	57	91

Note: *'Auditors Agreed' column is expressed as a percentage of the companies which have departed (i.e. of those in the 'Departed' column).

Table 2.7 Departures from standards to ensure true and fair

	Respondents	Willing to		Departed		Auditors Agreed*	
		No.	%	No.	%	No.	%
Parents	325	316	98	113	35	99	91
Subsidiaries	111	95	89	27	24	19	79
All Respondents	436	411		140	32	118	89

Note: *'Auditors Agreed' column is expressed as a percentage of the companies which have departed (i.e. of those in the 'Departed' column).

Table 2.8 Auditors have persuaded directors against intended departures

	Respondents	Persuasion on Law		Persuasion on Standards	
		No.	%	No.	%
Parents	330	11	3	19	6
Subsidiaries	111	0	0	6	5
All Respondents	441	11	2	25	6

The 'Auditors Agreed' columns in Tables 2.6 and 2.7 show the proportions of departures that have been accepted by auditors. Subsidiaries appear to disagree with their auditors more, though the number of cases involved is very small. A related finding, reported in Table 2.8, is that very few intended departures have been stopped by persuasion from auditors.

LIMITATIONS

All forms of research have their limitations. Perhaps the most important in the case of surveys is the danger of non-response bias. Our test for non-response bias was conducted on the basis of the size of companies (as measured by sales). It might have been expected that larger companies would respond either more willingly or less willingly than smaller companies, and that this would affect our results if the two groups gave different answers. However, the average rank (out of 900) of respondent companies was not statistically significantly different from the average rank of the whole population, at the five per cent level. So, for the most obviously relevant characteristic of companies, there seems to have been no non-response bias.

Industrial classification might have been another way of testing for bias but, for very large companies, classification is difficult and arbitrary, and no theory is obvious about why particular industries should not respond.

Ball and Foster (1982, p. 206) usefully list some of the problems relating to survey responses and other forms of research. They are:

1 the true motives of the respondents may be disguised;
2 past decisions may be rationalized;
3 it may be unclear exactly who, within an organization, is responsible for a specific decision; and
4 the responses may be intended as signals rather than as factual statements.

We are aware of these limitations but do not believe that they under-mine our survey results, since our hypotheses are expressed in terms of what finance directors claim to do rather than what they actually do.

A further limitation is that *The Times 1000* ranking omits financial and property companies; this somewhat reduces the generalizability of our findings. Also, internal consistency was not perfect, as discussed above and in note 2.

CONCLUSIONS

The survey questionnaire received a high response rate, so that the con-clusions below may be taken to be representative of directors of large UK companies. With respect to the seven hypotheses outlined earlier, the following conclusions seem reliable (with 95 per cent confidence intervals shown; parametric and non-parametric statistics are used, see note 4).

H_1: It seems possible to accept the hypothesis that the majority of direc-tors take no specific actions to ensure truth and fairness (though not quite with 95 per cent confidence for the parent sub-sample): Table 2.5 shows that those taking no specific steps are 52 per cent (±5 per cent) for parents and 66 per cent (±9 per cent) for subsidiaries.

H_2: From Tables 2.1–2.4 it may be seen that reliance on auditors is the most important technique for checking compliance with the rules. However, Tables 2.3 and 2.4 report slightly less reliance for 'true and fair'. Thus it is possible to accept a hypothesis that over 50 per cent of finance directors rely on auditors, but not that they rely *solely* on auditors.

H_3: Table 2.5 allows us to accept the hypothesis that over 50 per cent of finance directors see 'true' as the same as 'fair'. This is so for 81 per cent (±4%) of parents and 88 per cent (±6 per cent) of subsidiaries. More cautiously, one could express this as meaning that directors were unable to envisage circumstances where it would be necessary to draw this distinction.

H_4: Table 2.7 suggests that only very few companies would not depart from standards to give a true and fair view (2 per cent ±1 per cent for parents, and 11 per cent ±6 per cent for subsidiaries). More surprisingly, Table 2.6 shows that some companies would not depart from the details of the law (29 per cent ±5 per cent for parents, and 45 per cent ±10 per cent for subsidiaries). This does not allow us to accept the hypothesis that the *majority* of directors appear to misunderstand their responsibilities, but would allow a hypothesis that 'some' do.

H_5 Tables 2.1 to 2.7 show that subsidiaries are:

- More likely to rely fully on auditors to comply with law.
- More likely to rely fully on auditors to comply with standards.
  More likely to rely fully on auditors to ensure 'true and fair'.
  More likely to see 'true' as the same as 'fair'.
- Less likely to take specific steps to ensure 'true and fair'.
- Less likely to give additional information.
- Less willing to depart from law and standards.
- Less likely to have departed from law and standards.
  More willing to disagree with auditors on departures.
  ($\bullet$ = significant at the 5 per cent level.)[4]
  This suggests that it is possible to accept the hypothesis that subsidiaries rely more heavily on auditors and take a more mechanical view of compliance.

H_6:   Table 2.5 suggests that a majority of companies (58 per cent ±5 per cent for parents, and 85 per cent ±7 per cent for subsidiaries) are required by their auditors to provide a statement that the annual accounts give a true and fair view. The difference between parents and subsidiaries is significant.

SUMMARY

In summary, we can say that directors of most large UK companies claim to take no specific actions to give a true and fair view, to rely more heavily on auditors than on any other technique of compliance, and not to distinguish between 'true' and 'fair'. Some directors appear to misunderstand their responsibilities. Large companies that are subsidiaries appear to rely more heavily on auditors and to be more mechanical in applying rules. Further work remains to be done on whether the size of companies is important for these results, and on the actions of auditors as opposed to directors.

APPENDIX 2.1

Extracts from British Companies Acts

1844 ‘ . . . the Directors . . . shall cause . . . a full and fair Balance Sheet to be made up . . . ’ (s.35).

1862 ‘The Auditors shall make a Report to the Members upon the Balance Sheet and Accounts, and in every such Report they shall state whether, in their Opinion, the Balance Sheet is a full and fair Balance Sheet, containing the Particulars required by these Regulations, and properly drawn up so as to exhibit a true and correct View of the State of the Company's Affairs . . . ’ (para. 94, Table A).

1879 (banking companies) ‘The auditor or auditors . . . shall state whether, in his or her opinion, the balance sheet . . . is a full and fair balance properly drawn up, so as to exhibit a true and correct view of the state of the company's affairs, as shown by the books of the company . . . ’ (s.7).

1900 ‘ . . . the auditors . . . shall state whether, in their opinion, the balance sheet . . . is properly drawn up so as to exhibit a true and correct view of the state of the company's affairs as shown by the books of the company . . . ’ (s.23).

1948 ‘(1) Every balance sheet of a company shall give a true and fair view of the state of affairs of the company as at the end of its financial year, and every profit and loss account of a company shall give a true and fair view of the profit or loss for the financial year. . . . (3) . . . the [detailed] requirements of [the 8th Schedule] shall be without prejudice either to the general requirements of subsection (1) of this section or to any other requirements of this Act’ (s.149, re-enacting s.13, Companies Act 1947).

1985 ‘(2) The balance sheet shall give a true and fair view of the state of affairs of the company as at the end of the financial year; and the profit and loss account shall give a true and fair view of the profit or loss of the company for the financial year.

(3) Subsection (2) overrides

(a) the requirements of Schedule 4, and

(b) all other requirements of this Act as to the matters to be included in a company's accounts or in notes to those accounts;

and accordingly the following two subsections have effect.

(4) If the balance sheet or profit and loss account drawn up in accordance with those requirements would not provide sufficient information to comply with subsection (2), any necessary additional information must be provided in that balance sheet or profit and loss account, or in a note to the accounts.

(5) If, owing to special circumstances, in the case of any company, compliance with any such requirement in relation to the balance sheet or profit and loss account would prevent compliance with subsection (2) (even if additional information were provided in accordance with subsection (4)), the directors shall depart from that requirement in preparing the balance sheet or profit and loss account (so far as necessary in order to comply with subsection (2)).

(6) If the directors depart from any such requirement, particulars of the departure, the reasons for it and its effect shall be given in a note to the accounts'.

(s.228 = re-enactment of S.149 of 1948 Act as amended by 1981 Act; s.230 provides similarly for group accounts.)

APPENDIX 2.2

Private and confidential

Questionnaire to Finance Directors for ICAEW Research Study
NAME OF RESPONDENT ....
NAME OF COMPANY ....
RESPONDENT'S POSITION IN COMPANY ....
DATE QUESTIONNAIRE COMPLETED ....

Questions

1 What do you do to ensure that your company's annual financial statements comply with the detailed accounting provisions of the Companies Act (for example, use checklist, rely on auditors, etc)?

2 What do you do to ensure that your annual financial statements comply with accounting standards?

3 Do you take any specific steps *in addition* to the above to ensure that the annual financial statements give a true and fair view? If so, please give details.   Yes/No

DETAILS:

4 Did the detailed formats and valuation rules introduced by the Companies Act 1981 lead your company to change any of the procedures it had established to ensure that the annual financial statements gave a true and fair view? If so, please give details.   Yes/No

DETAILS:

5 To what extent does your company rely upon the auditors to ensure compliance with:

(a) the detailed provisions of the Companies Act;
(b) accounting standards;
(c) the requirement to give a true and fair view?

	Fully Relies	Partly Relies	Not at all
Companies Act provisions			
accounting standards			
true and fair view			

6   In deciding whether or not the annual financial statements of your company are true and fair, do you distinguish between what is 'true' and what is 'fair'? If so, please give details.   Yes/No

DETAILS:

7(a) Would your company be willing to depart from an accounting standard if this were necessary in order to give a true and fair view?
                                                                        Yes/No

  (b) Has your company done so within the last five years?
                                                                        Yes/No

  (c) If 'yes', please give the year or some details. Also, were you able to persuade the auditors that it was necessary to do so?
                                                                        Yes/No

8   Within the last five years have you ever wished to depart from an accounting standard in order to give a true and fair view but been persuaded by your auditors not to do so?   Yes/No

9(a) Would your company be willing to depart from one of the detailed provisions of the Companies Act if this were necessary in order to give a true and fair view?   Yes/No

  (b) Has your company done so within the last five years?   Yes/No

  (c) If 'Yes', were you able to persuade the company's auditors that it was necessary to do so?   Yes/No

10   Within the last five years have you ever wished to depart from one of the detailed provisions of the Companies Act in order to give a true and fair view but been persuaded by your auditors not to do so?
                                                                        Yes/No

11   Within the last five years, has your company supplied, in order to give a true and fair view, information *additional* to that required by the detailed provisions of the Companies Act and by accounting standards?
                                                                        Yes/No

     If 'yes', please give one example.

12   Do the auditors require from your company each year a statement that, in the directors' opinion, the accounts give a true and fair view?

Yes/No

13   If you wish to provide us with any further information relating to your company's experience of giving a true and fair view please do so below, preferably with examples.

NOTES

1 The requirement to give a true and fair view extends to a number of organizations not registered under the Companies Acts (Williams, 1985, pp. 25–6) some of which, e.g. the Port of London Authority and the Post Office, are included in *The Times 1000* and thus in our survey. In all, 72 per cent of the respondents were ultimate parents, 24 per cent subsidiaries and 4 per cent non-Companies Act.

2 For example, only 0.4 per cent of companies said that they would not be prepared to depart from a standard, but later reported that they had departed. Similarly, only 0.2 per cent said that they fully relied on auditors, yet also said that they had departed from standards without the agreement of auditors. However, a comparison of claims relating to reliance on auditors shows a consistently higher reliance in Tables 2.3 and 2.4 than in Tables 2.1 and 2.2. For example, 77 per cent of parents mention auditors in Table 2.1 whereas 86 per cent suggest full or partial reliance on auditors (for Companies Act matters) in Table 2.3. This may be because directors only bothered to mention fairly substantial reliance in the answers analyzed in Tables 2.1 and 2.2.

3 In all tables, percentages refer to the number of respondents to a particular question. All questions had a high response rate.

4 Given the very large sample sizes, parametric statistics might be thought to be satisfactory. However, for added comfort, chi-squared statistics were also calculated for the 13 comparisons involved in H_5 and H_6. In all 13 cases, the same conclusions were reached as for parametric statistics. For example, for the first four comparisons in H_6, the decision criterion using chi-squares is 3.84. The chi-square calculations yield 12.48, 6.73, 1.14 and 2.36, respectively. As with parametric statistics, this suggests significance for the first two only. These are without Yates' correction, but the same conclusions are reached with such a correction.

REFERENCES

Ball, R. and Foster, G. (1982), 'Corporate financial reporting: a methodological review of empirical research', *Journal of Accounting Research. Supplement*, pp. 161–234.

Baumol, W.J. (1986), *Superfairness. Applications and Theory* (Cambridge, Mass: The MIT Press).

Carmichael, D.R. and Winters, A.J. (1982), 'The evolution of audit reporting', in Nichols, D.R. and Stettler, H.F. (eds), *Auditing Symposium VI* (Lawrence: School of Business, University of Kansas).

Chastney, J.G. (1975), *True and Fair View – History, Meaning and the Impact of the Fourth Directive* (London: Institute of Chartered Accountants in England and Wales).

Cowan, T.K. (1965), 'Are truth and fairness generally acceptable?', *Accounting Review* (October), pp. 788–94.

Dhaliwal, D.S., Salamon, G. and Smith, E.D. (1982), 'The effect of owner versus management control on the choice of accounting methods', *Journal of Accounting and Economics* (July), pp. 41–53.

Flint, D. (1982), *A True and Fair View in Company Accounts* (Edinburgh: Institute of Chartered Accountants of Scotland).

Griffiths, I. (1986), *Creative Accounting*, (London: Sidgwick and Jackson).

Harris, N.G.E. (1987), 'Fairness in financial reporting', *Journal of Applied Philosophy*, vol. 4, no. 1.

Hoffman, G. and Arden, M. (1983), 'Counsel's opinion on true and fair', *Accountancy* (November), pp. 154–6.

Hopkins, L. (1984), *The Audit Report* (London: Butterworth).

Jensen, M.C. and Meckling, W.H. (1976), 'Theory of the firm: managerial behavior, agency costs and ownership structure', *Journal of Financial Economics* (October), pp. 305–60.

Law Society (1986), *Off-Balance Sheet Finance and Window Dressing*, Memorandum by The Law Society's Standing Committee on Company Law (June).

Parker, R.H. (1989), 'Importing and exporting accounting: the British experience', in Hopwood, A.G. (ed.), *International Pressures for Accounting Change* (London: Prentice-Hall International).

Rawls, J. (1972), *A Theory of Justice* (Oxford: Clarendon Press).

Rutherford, B.A. (1983), ' "Spoilt beauty": the true and fair doctrine in translation', *AUTA Review* (Spring), pp. 33–6.

Rutteman, P. (1984), *The EEC accounting directives and their effects* (University College, Cardiff).

Times (1985), *The Times 1000, 1985–86* (London: Times Books).

Tweedie, D.P. and Kellas, J. (1987), 'Off-balance sheet financing', *Accountancy* (April), pp. 91–5.

Williams, D.W. (1985), 'Legal perspectives on auditing', in Kent, D., Sherer, M. and Turley, S. (eds), *Current Issues in Auditing* (London: Harper and Row).

Zmijewski, M. and Hagerman, R. (1981), 'An income strategy approach to the positive theory of accounting standard-setting choice', *Journal of Accounting and Economics* (August), pp. 129–49.

This paper by C.W. Nobes and R.H. Parker was first published in the Journal of Business Finance & Accounting, *April 1991.*

3 'True and Fair'

UK Auditors' View

ABSTRACT

An earlier paper surveyed the behaviour of finance directors of the 900 largest UK companies with respect to giving a true and fair view in annual accounts. This present paper results from personal interviews with technical partners of all the twenty largest UK auditing firms (which includes the auditors of nearly all the companies in the previous survey). The paper examines the operational meaning of 'true and fair' to large auditing firms, and how it fits into the context of law and standards. It is concluded that one effect of the requirement as it works in practice is to give support to auditors' views in areas not yet covered by accounting standards. Contrasts emerge between the interpretations of directors and those of auditors.

INTRODUCTION

The actions of financial directors of large UK companies with respect to ensuring truth and fairness of annual accounts are examined by Nobes and Parker (1991). This present paper is concerned with the actions of the *auditors* of large companies. In addition to discovering what auditors do (or what they say they do), we compare the differing ways in which directors and auditors interpret true and fair in practice.

It has been the duty of the auditors of UK companies since 1948 to report on whether or not the financial statements they have audited give a true and fair view (TFV). The giving of a true and fair view is also required by other legislation, for example that applying to the Port of London Authority and the Post Office (Williams, 1985, pp. 25–6). The precise requirement as to true and fair was amended in 1981 and again in 1989. At the time of our survey the relevant legislation was contained in s.228 of the Companies Act 1985. Under this section the obligation to give a TFV overrides the detailed accounting requirements of the Act. If financial statements drawn up in compliance with those requirements do not provide sufficient information to give a TFV, additional information must be given. If compliance plus additional information still does not give a TFV, the detailed requirements of the Act must be departed from. No reference was made in law to compliance with accounting standards.[1] Despite the importance of the TFV concept, the Act provides neither a nominal nor an operational definition, and this gap has not been filled by decided cases. Nominal definitions of true and fair are discussed in, for example, Chastney (1975), Flint (1982), Harris (1987) and Nobes and Parker (1991), but no consensus has been reached.

This is a paper about both truth and fairness and the audit process. It is not our purpose to ask why companies are required to be audited or why they should be required to make detailed accounting disclosures or to give a true and fair view. These are all taken as given. We treat auditing as a technical activity and do not concern ourselves directly with the rationales for auditing, which can be derived from information economics or agency theory, with the structure of the market for auditing services, or with the sociology of the auditing profession. Nevertheless, we hope that our results may be of interest to researchers in these areas especially insofar as we comment on the possible difference of approach to TFV of the Big Eight and the 'Next Twelve' and the way in which the audit of truth and fairness may affect the relationship between a company's directors and its auditors.

RESEARCH DESIGN

We carried out our research by means of a questionnaire (reproduced in Appendix 3.3) and structured interviews with the 'Top Twenty' UK audit firms[2] at the date of our survey. The Top Twenty was taken as representing the largest UK firms. Although relative rankings within the Top Twenty (as reported in *Accountancy*) changed over the period of our two surveys, the constituent firms remained constant, as indeed they have since, apart from mergers which have reduced the number to seventeen.

In order to enable an approximate comparison with our directors' survey of the top 900 companies in the *Times 1000 1985/86*, it was necessary to determine the auditors of these companies. An investigation of the majority[3] of these established that over 80 per cent were audited by the largest fourteen firms. We believe, therefore, that our survey of the largest twenty firms at that date captures nearly all the relevant auditors.

One criticism of questionnaire surveys (such as that in Nobes and Parker, 1991) is that there is too much scope for misunderstanding by respondents, misinterpretation of responses by researchers, and general loss of nuance. However, with a survey of 900 directors, a more personal approach would have been impractical. By contrast, for this present survey, we were able to carry out personal interviews, ranging in length from one to three hours, with representatives of all of the then top twenty firms. That is, this can be seen not as a sample, but as a survey of the whole population of the twenty largest firms, with no non-response. In the case of each firm, we interviewed a technical partner, or some equivalent such as the director of technical services. In several cases, more than one partner or other staff member was present. In all cases, it was made clear that we wished to discuss listed and other large clients with which the interviewees were familiar (see below).

It is possible to argue that technical partners are atypical members of large firms. It is the audit partners not the technical partners who sign audit reports. Moreover, it is often argued that technical partners are less likely to share the view of their clients[4] and to accept accounting policies favourable to clients than are audit partners. There is certainly anecdotal evidence to this effect. However, any one interviewee would be atypical; and the advantage of technical partners is that they usually have considerable experience with their firms and that they are more likely to be familiar with the interesting cases that test the meaning of the TFV.

The interviews were mainly carried out in summer 1989, before the enactment of the Companies Act 1989 which made small changes to the TFV requirement (now s.226 of the Companies Act 1985 as amended) and introduced a large number of detailed rules concerning group accounting. That is, there had been no significant changes in rules between our directors' and auditors' surveys.

In order to draft a questionnaire on the actions and views of auditors we examined:

1 the Auditing Standards and Guidelines issued by the Auditing Practices Committee (APC) of the Consultative Committee of Accountancy Bodies (CCAB);
2 the published audit manuals of leading UK accountancy firms;
3 the results of our survey of UK financial directors.

The questionnaire was then refined by pilot interviews (at which both researchers were present) with the technical partners and other technical staff of two large accountancy firms.

The references to true and fair in the Auditing Standards and Guidelines are of a general nature only. The original (1980) auditing standard on the Audit Report (current at the date of our survey) stated that, when expressing an opinion that financial statements give a true and fair view, the auditor should be satisfied, *inter alia*, that:

1 all relevant Statements of Standard Practice (SSAPs) have been complied with, except in situations in which for justifiable reasons they are not strictly applicable because they are impracticable or, exceptionally, having regard to the circumstances, would be inappropriate or give a misleading view; and

2 any significant accounting policies which are not the subject of SSAPs are appropriate to the circumstances of the business.

The standard does not state that a TFV can be achieved by adherence to SSAPs but it does appear to suggest that they are of the utmost importance. The Accounting Standards Committee was set up in part in order to 'give a more definitive approach to the concept of what gives a true and fair view' (Flint, 1982, p. 22). The relationship between accounting standards and TFV is complex, as is shown later in this paper. Perceptions of truth and fairness may be influenced both by existing standards and by standards in the making.

The large UK auditing firms all have links with auditing firms in the USA. The approximate American equivalent of TFV is 'present fairly in conformity with generally accepted accounting principles'. US auditors are required by Statement on Auditing Standards No. 5 to make judgments as to whether the accounting principles selected and applied have general acceptance and are appropriate in the circumstances; the financial statements including the related notes are informative of matters that may affect their use, understanding and interpretation; the information in the financial statements is classified and summarized in a manner that is neither too detailed nor too condensed; and the financial statements present the financial position, results of operations and changes in financial position within a range of acceptable limits.

Audit manuals make few explicit references to a true and fair view. All those inspected refer to true and fair as a legal obligation and as a component of the opinion paragraph of the audit report. Reporting on truth and fairness is stated to be the primary objective of an audit. The only manual, so far as we could ascertain, which attempts an operational definition of truth and fairness for an auditor is that of Coopers & Lybrand (1986/7, section 101.05; see Appendix 3.1 for quotations). It is said to be implicit that substance should take precedence over form as part of giving a TFV. In particular (section 810.13):

1 Accounts which mislead, or potentially mislead, cannot give a true and fair view.

2 Artificial transactions should not be accounted for as though they were real.

3 There has to be proper accounting and disclosure of liabilities, contingent liabilities and commitments.

The manual states (section 101.08) that following a SSAP might give a misleading view but does not give an example.

The Neville Russell audit manual (1988, Part 1, p. 230) states firmly that true and fair defies definition but that consideration of truth and fairness will include consideration of the appropriateness and consistency of the accounting policies adopted, whether the amounts at which assets, liabilities, profits and losses are stated are 'fair', whether all significant information has been disclosed, whether the financial statements are presented in a manner which 'assists the readers' understanding of the statements as a whole, bearing in mind the relative importance of individual items', and whether relevant SSAPs have been observed.

The results of our earlier financial directors' survey can be summarized as follows:

1 The majority of directors take no *specific* actions to ensure truth and fairness.

2 Directors rely heavily on auditors to check compliance with the detailed rules of company law and accounting standards and less heavily on auditors to check compliance with the requirement to give a true and fair view.

3 The majority of directors regard 'true' as the same as 'fair'.

4 Very few directors would not depart from standards in order to give a true and fair view.

5 Some directors would not depart from the detailed rules of the Companies Act in order to give a true and fair view.

6 A majority of companies are required by their auditors to provide a statement that the annual financial statements give a true and fair view.

It is the directors not the auditors who are responsible for ensuring that the accounts give a TFV. To what extent do auditors rely upon the directors? To do so entirely would make the audit report worthless; not to do so at all would seem to be very difficult. A reading of the audit manuals suggests that some, but not all, audit firms require directors to state in a letter of representation that the financial statements give a TFV. There is no mention, however, of a TFV in the draft letter of representation in the Auditing Guideline on 'Representations by Management'.

Since there is a clear responsibility in the Companies Act for the directors to produce true and fair accounts, it can be argued that a formal representation by them that they have done so is of minor importance. On the other hand, the lack of any mention in the annual report of a TFV other than in the auditors' report may suggest to readers that it is the auditors not the directors who are primarily responsible for the truth and fairness of the financial statements.

Is 'truth' distinguishable from 'fairness'? This is not a point discussed by most manuals. An earlier version of the Coopers & Lybrand manual (1981, p. 10), however, stated that the words 'true and fair view' were intended to be read together. Hopkins (1984, pp. 50–1) reproduces a Pannell Kerr Forster diagram which distinguishes between 'truth', 'fairness' and 'compliance with legislation and standards'. Our previous survey disclosed that most financial directors do not make a distinction.

On the basis of our reading of the Auditing Standards and Guidelines, the audit firm manuals, and the conclusions of our financial directors survey, our expectations were as below. All references to 'audit firms' are, unless otherwise stated, to the top twenty audit firms in the UK at the date of our survey.

1 Audit firms do not carry out any procedures to test TFV which are separate from those used to test compliance with the detailed provisions of the Companies Act and accounting standards.
2 The increasing complexity of company legislation and accounting standards has not led audit firms to change their procedures with respect to TFV.
3 Audit firms do not distinguish between what is 'true' and what is 'fair'.
4 Audit firms rely partly on a client's directors to ensure that the accounts give a true and fair view.
5 Audit firms do not require client companies to state that in the directors' opinion the accounts give a true and fair view.

At the time of our survey the Big Eight formed a clearly identifiable class of very large multinational accountancy firms. Because of their size, prestige, high profile and a client base more biased towards large listed companies, it could be argued that they are able to exert more pressure on clients, take a more sophisticated view of TFV or be more vulnerable to litigation in cases where TFV was in doubt. The US literature certainly advances this view. Dopuch and Simunic (1982) suggested a two-tier market structure for audit, in which the Big Eight were more competent, more independent, or both. De Angelo (1981) links audit firm size to investment in reputation and hence to expected quality and independence. Wallace (1980) and Benston (1985) suggest that the

Big Eight are more competent and credible. We therefore further expected:

6 There is a difference between the actions of the Big Eight audit firms and the 'Next Twelve' UK audit firms.

These six expectations determined questions 1, 2, 3, 6, 9, 11, 12, 13 and 14 in our questionnaire (see Appendix 3.3). Questions 4, 5, 7, 8 and 10 were added to enable additional comparisons to be made with the results of our financial directors' survey.

We deliberately did not ask our respondents to provide us with a nominal definition of true and fair. Our interest in this paper is in how UK auditors operate the TFV requirement in practice. In the final section we attempt to identify the importance of the TFV requirement, and to suggest the role it plays in contemporary UK financial reporting.

SURVEY RESULTS

The survey included fourteen closed-ended questions, the results of which are shown in Table 3.1 for all twenty firms. Appendix 3.2 repeats these results, but shows the Big Eight separately (the survey was carried

Table 3.1 Responses to closed-ended questions (see Appendix 3.3 for full questions)

Question	Yes Yes	Partly	Yes and No*	No
1 Separate procedures to check TFV?	9		11	
2 Did 1981 Act change procedures for TFV?	5			15
3 Do you distinguish 'true' from 'fair'?	16			4
4 Has client wished to depart from a standard to give TFV?	15			5
5 Has firm persuaded client to depart from a standard?	4			16
7 Has client wished to depart from detailed legal provisions to give TFV?	14			6
8 Has firm persuaded client to depart from detailed legal provisions?	8			12
9 Does Act contain obstructions to TFV?	8			12
10 Has client provided additional information to give TFV?	19			1
11 Have standards changed procedures for TFV?	6		3	11
12 Does firm rely on directors for TFV?	0	16	4	0
13 Does firm require letter from directors on TFV?	6			14
14 Should law change to require directors to state TFV?	14			6

Note: *Responses were classified as 'Yes and No' when the answer was 'yes' for some aspects but 'no' for others; see text under 'Survey Results'.

out before the mergers of 1989/90). As reported below, we examined whether the Big Eight were different from the Next Twelve. The responses are discussed by subject in the paragraphs that follow, and this includes answers to the open-ended questions (no. 6 and 'further particulars' relating to several closed-ended questions).

Separate procedures to test true and fair

Our expectation was that audit firms do not carry out any procedures which are separate from those used to test compliance with the detailed provisions of the Companies Act and accounting standards. Table 3.1 shows that nine firms answered 'yes' to question 1 about the existence of specific procedures. However, in nearly all cases, the 'yes' related to a review by a second partner for all listed companies or sensitive cases, where one of the second partner's particular duties was to check for TFV. For example, one respondent replied that a 'Second audit partner [is] required on certain larger clients, who are more likely to present such a problem. Partner's responsibilities include review of accounts and all potentially contentious areas.' Another indicated that there was an overall review of the accounts for 'reasonableness' and a consideration of the impact of large, unusual and related party transactions. As the eleven 'yes and no' answers indicate, our respondents found difficulty in giving a simple answer to this question. For example, one of these respondents stated that 'Whilst we have no "procedures" as such we believe that manager/partner review of accruing and unusual transactions, including reference to our National Technical Department on points of difficulty, picks up "truth and fairness" problems. We believe that an understanding of the business and transactions involved will highlight potential problems.' Another reported the existence of an independent team whose function was to challenge *all* audit opinions.

We also expected that the increasing complexity of company legislation and accounting standards has not led audit firms to change their procedures with respect to TFV. The responses to question 2 show that most firms had not changed their procedures for checking for TFV as a result of the enormous expansion of legal accounting rules introduced by the Companies Act 1981, apart of course from adding many points to a compliance checklist. In some ways one might have thought that there was now less need to check for TFV but, since the 'specific' checks mentioned are rather vague, the lack of change after 1981 is not surprising. One respondent noted that the Act encourages a 'rule book' approach.

A slightly larger number of respondents reported that the gradual expansion of *standards* had caused a change in procedures for checking TFV, beyond merely adding more details to a compliance checklist (question 11). Those respondents who explained the change reported that there was now *less* need to check for TFV because of the reduced flexibility brought about by the standards programme. The increase in the number of standards had 'minimized the area of argument'.

More subtly, several respondents suggested that the meaning of TFV had changed as a result of standards. As one technical partner put it, '"true and fair" moves on and takes on additional dimensions with each accounting standard'. For example, it would not now be 'true and fair' if finance leases were uncapitalized; presentation has become more capable of being unfair; ED49 ('Reflecting the substance of transactions') would lead to major changes if it became a standard. Another respondent stated that as a result of standards users have higher expectations but there was more scope for 'loop-holing' (i.e. following the letter rather than the spirit of a standard).

Truth as opposed to fairness

We did not expect that audit firms would distinguish between what is 'true' and what is 'fair'. In fact a large majority of respondents could and did distinguish between truth and fairness (question 3). Of those four who draw no distinction, two said that they *could* make a distinction but did not do so in practice. Of those who distinguish, four mentioned that normally the expression is a portmanteau, including one who noted that the portmanteau expression means more than the sum of its parts. Several respondents volunteered that 'fair' was more important than 'true'; none suggested the reverse. Interpretations of the words by our respondents are given in Table 3.2. 'Fair' is given a more diverse interpretation than 'true'. Walker (1984, p. 20) argues that it may not be that 'true and fair' is more than the sum of its parts but that it means something different from its parts. This was not suggested by any of our respondents.

Additional information

One way of distinguishing operationally between 'truth' and 'fairness' would be to report 'truth' (i.e. the form) in the financial statements and to add 'fairness' (i.e. the substance) in the Notes. None of our respondents put the position as simply and crudely as this, but a very obvious effect of the TFV requirement is the need to give additional information

Table 3.2 Respondents' interpretation of 'true' and 'fair'

True	Fair
Based on fact	Not misleading (three times)
Undistorted facts	Substance over form (twice)
Correct	Proper reflection
Complies with rules	Putting in right context
Not in conflict with facts	Consistent with underlying reality
Objective	Ability to understand what has
Correct, within materiality	really gone on
Adherence to events	In accordance with rules in context
Factual accuracy	Reasonable
	Gives right impression
	Whether reader receives right message

Table 3.3 Examples of extra disclosures required to give TFV

Pro forma statements for off-balance sheet finance (six times)
Sale and commitment to repurchase (twice)
Amplification of unusual or exceptional circumstances
Recoverability of ACT
Nature of extraordinaries
Currency exposure
Disclosure of *ex gratia* compensation
Details of unconsolidated uncontrolled foreign 'subsidiaries' or 'associates'
Method of taking profit on long-term contracts
Pro forma concerning post-year-end acquisition
Related party transactions
Contingencies and commitments
Pension contribution holiday
Value of buildings for a non-going concern

to that which the rules directly require (question 10). The giving of additional information is, as might be expected, more frequent than departures. All but one of the respondents could think of examples of additional information, for most of them including cases where the firm had to encourage or persuade the client to disclose. Table 3.3 summarizes the extra disclosures deemed necessary.

The extra disclosures are most common in controversial areas not yet explicitly covered by law or standard. Various areas of 'creative accounting' such as off-balance-sheet finance and sale and commitment to repurchase are well to the fore. Another example is related party transactions.

Departures from law and standards

Most firms (15 and 14 respectively) reported that various clients had wished to depart from standards and from law in order to give a TFV in the previous five years (questions 4 and 7). Two firms said that the potential 'law breakers'[5] had been dissuaded. Our respondents' examples of the reasons for these departures are given in Table 3.4. Nevertheless, these examples were said to be rare. A distinction can be made between (i) 'general' departures from the law (those made by nearly all companies, usually where compliance with a SSAP resulted in possible contravention of a detailed provision of the Companies Act), and (ii) 'specific departures' (those arising from problems peculiar to a particular company). Minor variations from prescribed balance sheet and profit and loss formats seem not to be regarded as departures.

Interestingly, some firms have had to encourage or persuade clients to depart from a standard (4 respondents to question 5) or a law (8 respondents to question 8). The examples (intended as illustrations not as a complete listing) supplied by our respondents are given in Table 3.5.

The examples given in Tables 3.4 and 3.5 are not easy to categorize but many of them fall into areas where standards are not yet in place because the area is relatively new (e.g. marking to market, off-balance-sheet schemes), controversial (e.g. aspects of the valuation of stocks and work in progress, off-balance-sheet schemes) or acceptable to accountants but not in accordance with the less flexible detailed legal rules introduced in 1981 (e.g. marking to market). The influence of overseas standards is also apparent (e.g. fully accounting for deferred tax).

As noted at the foot of Table 3.4 some standards specifically require the details of the law to be departed from. Some of the departures from law relate to standards that have since been amended to comply with the letter of the law, for example, as in SSAP 9 (revised), by re-defining work-in-progress as 'amounts recoverable on contracts'.[6]

Perceived significance of TFV

The responses reported above suggest that the TFV, in some cases, has a major impact on financial reporting, and that auditors can be significant in the process. Most respondents thought that TFV can be a powerful means of overriding detailed legal provisions (question 6). Some thought that nothing was excluded from its scope, and others that there was little

Table 3.4 Examples of causes of departure from standards and law

Standards departed from	Details of law departed from*
Extraordinary and exceptional items (three times) (SSAP 6)	Formats; distinction of liabilities and capital (twice)
Taking profit before contract agreed (twice) (SSAP 2)	Taking unrealized profits (twice)
Base stock for sugar (twice) (SSAP 9)	Refusal to disclose information
Non-revaluation of investment property (twice) (SSAP 19)	Netting expenses and revenues
Lack of significant influence over an overseas 'associate' (SSAP 1)	Non-consolidation of a subsidiary
Non-material item treated as exceptional (SSAP 6)	Consolidation of a non-subsidiary
Prior year items (SSAP 6)	
Stocks of tea at realized values (SSAP 9)	
Stocks of wool at selling price less costs (SSAP 9)	
Marking to market (SSAP 9)	
Use of completion method on long-term contracts (SSAP 9)	
Taking profit on short-term contracts (before revision of SSAP 9)	
Lack of funds flow statement (SSAP 10)	
Non-depreciation of buildings (SSAP 12)	
Fully accounting for deferred tax (SSAP 15)	

Note: *Some standards specifically require the detail of the law to be departed from (e.g. SSAP 19, SSAP 20). These have been ignored here.

Table 3.5 Examples of reasons for persuading clients to depart from standards or law

Standards	Law
Marking to market: valuation (twice) (SSAP 9)	In order to correct for an off-balance-sheet scheme (three times)
Dates of acquisition and disposal for consolidation (SSAP 14)	Marking to market: profit
	Treatment of contract work-in-progress

agreement on which matters might be excluded: group structure and directors' disclosures were suggested. According to one respondent, s.228(3) of the Companies Act 1985 simply means that 'accounts must be first and foremost true and fair rather than prepared in accordance with predetermined rules'. On the other hand, one technical partner was clear that the section does not give directors 'an open ended option to disregard the detailed measurement, presentation and disclosure requirements of the Act'.

Nearly half the respondents thought that the law contained some obstructions to giving a TFV (question 9). Some thought that it merely enabled directors to hide behind the law; some that the law sometimes made the TFV very difficult for auditors and directors. Too many details in the Act, said one respondent, can drive out fairness. A second mentioned the danger of 'unthinking compliance' and a third considered that the rules could be 'easily subverted'. The most frequently mentioned problems were connected to the definition of subsidiaries in the Companies Act 1985 before its amendment in 1989. However, with the new definitions and with the strengthening of the TFV[7] introduced by the 1989 Act, these problems may be reduced. It must be said that the Accounting Standards Committee frequently met legal objections to its plans; e.g. in 1989 on government grants and on marking to market (see Nobes, 1990).

Auditors' relationships with directors

Unsurprisingly, no audit firms said that they fully relied on directors to ensure a TFV, and none said that they put no reliance on directors (question 12). Those respondents who explained further said that they relied on directors for some estimates and for internal knowledge, particularly as the clients had many qualified accountants working for them. Nevertheless, the directors' answers are reviewed and tested. Directors are not relied upon if there is experience of difficulty with them or if the auditors feel uncomfortable about their reliability. More reliance is placed on directors where internal control systems are seen to be good. Thus some auditors rely on some directors for some aspects of TFV.

A minority of the audit firms (six) require directors to commit themselves in writing to the fact that their accounts give a TFV (question 13). One respondent stated that his firm was opposed to such a statement on the grounds that it would make the auditor feel too secure. However, a majority (fourteen) thought that directors should be required by law to state publicly the truth and fairness of their accounts (question 14). It would, suggested one respondent, 'concentrate the mind'. Another thought such a requirement would be less useful for large companies where the directors are 'more likely to understand their responsibilities and therefore the significance of their signatures on the accounts'. A third thought it unnecessary since the directors already sign the accounts. Another respondent stated, however, that it was his firm's experience that 'many view this as little more than authorising the release of the accounts for distribution to shareholders, or, even worse, an auditor-imposed requirement'. It might be thought curious that some auditors would like a change in the law to ensure public confirmation of a TFV but have not yet asked for private confirmation. A possible explanation is that the latter is regarded as part of the gathering of audit evidence whereas the former is seen as a question of the directors' responsibility to the shareholders (Chandler, 1983). As already noted, the draft letter of representation in Auditing Guideline on 'Representations by Management' does not mention truth and fairness.

Big Eight v. Next Twelve

We expected to find a difference between the actions of the Big Eight and the Next Twelve UK audit firms. The disaggregated survey data in Appendix 3.2 were used to calculate the results for the ten yes/no questions shown in Table 3.6. Of these questions, the Big Eight responded 'yes' more often than the Next Twelve for all questions,[8] except for equal response on question 2. It is noteworthy, however, that except for questions 8 and 9 the Big Eight and the Next Twelve were in agreement in either giving a majority of 'yes' answers or a majority of 'no' answers.

Table 3.6 Big Eight and Next Twelve

Questions (see Table 3.1)	Big 8 'Yes' %	Next 12 'Yes' %
2	25	25
3	87.5	75
4	87.5	66.7
5	25	16.7
7	87.5	58.3
8	62.5	25
9	50	33.3
10	100	91.7
13	37.5	25
14	87.5	58.3

Question 8 concerned 'persuading' clients to depart from detailed legal provisions. The results suggest that the Big Eight (62.5 per cent 'yes') have more persuasive power or perhaps more need to persuade (because of the size and complexity of their clients' activities) than the Next Twelve (25 per cent 'yes'). Both the Big Eight and the Next Twelve gave more 'yes' answers than 'no' answers to those questions (4, 7 and 10) which refer mainly to clients wishing to depart and providing additional information. Not surprisingly, larger firms found it easier to provide examples for the four questions mentioned in this paragraph (and question 5), because they have more large clients.

Question 9 asked whether the law was thought to contain potential obstructions to TFV. Half the Big Eight thought so, but only a third of the Next Twelve. Question 14 asked whether the law should be changed to require directors to state that the accounts give a TFV. This received more support from the Big Eight (87.5 per cent) than from the Next Twelve (58.3 per cent).

DIRECTORS AND AUDITORS: A COMPARISON

Some of the questions asked in the survey of directors reported in Nobes and Parker (1991) are directly comparable to the auditors' questions reported on here; these are summarized in Table 3.7.

The most interesting difference of opinion concerns whether 'true' can be distinguished from 'fair'. Among finance directors, only 17 per cent distinguish, whereas 80 per cent of the auditors distinguish (with half of the remainder also saying that they would be able to distinguish). Although most finance directors are qualified accountants, their approach to TFV differs significantly in this respect from that of technical audit partners. It is suggested in Nobes and Parker (1991) that the reason that

Table 3.7 Directors and auditors

	Directors %	Auditors %
'Opinions'		
Distinguish between true and fair	17	80
'Facts'		
Client* departed from law for TFV	14	70
Client* departed from standard for TFV	32	75
Client* has provided more information for TFV	32	95
Directors provide statement on TFV	65	30

* As explained in the text, the auditors are reporting on a range of clients.

most directors did not make a true/fair distinction was that they were rule-oriented. This implies that the major cause of the difference between auditors and directors is that auditors have a different interpretation of fair from that of directors, rather than a different interpretation of true.

The other four topics examined in Table 3.7 concern matters of fact. The first three relate to departures and the provision of additional information. The auditors' percentages are markedly higher than the finance directors'. This is to be expected: finance directors were answering a question referring to their own company; auditors could draw upon the experience of all the clients of the firm. The great majority of auditors reported that clients had departed from laws and standards in order to give a TFV, and nearly all reported examples of additional information being given. Not surprisingly, these examples known to the auditors seem to come from a minority of companies, as Table 3.7 suggests.

The final comparison is hard to explain: 65 per cent of directors say that they provide statements to the auditors confirming a TFV, whereas only 30 per cent of the firms say that they ask clients for one. This could in principle be explained if auditors with more large clients than average were more likely to ask for such statements. Indeed, Table 3.6 shows that a larger proportion of Big Eight auditors (37.5 per cent) than Next Twelve auditors (25 per cent) do ask for statements, but this difference is obviously not large enough to explain the discrepancy. A tentative explanation is that directors were referring to informal statements and auditors to formal statements. An alternative (unlikely) explanation is that such statements declined in popularity in the short period between the two surveys.[9]

THE IMPORTANCE OF TRUE AND FAIR

Our survey results and subsequent discussions with our respondents suggest that the TFV requirement is used by auditors as a means of obtaining compliance not only with extant law and standards but also with auditors' views of what the laws or standards ought to be on issues which are so new or so controversial that there is as yet no established rule. Less often, it is used by auditors to modify, in the interests of what they perceive as fairness, rules already established. Insisting on a TFV provides an argument more quickly and readily available to the auditor than changes in the detail of a law or standard (although this may happen, as it has in the case of controlled non-subsidiaries). TFV is, in a sense, an article of belief, a credo, a symbol. It is in this context that we accept the suggestion of a lawyer (Williams,

1985, p. 30) that the TFV requirement exists mainly for the benefit of auditors.

Whether or not directors find the use of TFV by auditors in their interests will depend upon the circumstances. Presumably the directors of investment companies do not disapprove of the use of the TFV override in SSAP 19. On the other hand, the evidence of our survey shows that the provision of additional information and departures from law or standards is sometimes the result of auditor pressure. Nevertheless it would also be possible for auditors to use TFV as an argument in favour of practices that directors wished to adopt.

TFV can thus be seen, especially in recent years, as a factor in the relationship between auditors and directors. It may often be in the interest of directors to stress legal form over economic substance. In this they may be encouraged by merchant bankers and lawyers. The controversy over off-balance-sheet financing has brought home clearly to auditors the danger of losing control of accounting. As one auditor has lamented:

> It is the legal profession which has seized control. It is the lawyer who determines what the accountants and auditors will do, how accounts are to be prepared and what is disclosed. . . . The auditor has become the servant of the lawyer and is no longer the master of his own destiny.
>
> (Brindle, 1987, p. 49)

Historically, the conjunction of 'true' and 'fair' in British law originated with the Institute of Chartered Accountants in England and Wales' witnesses to the Cohen Committee on Company Law Amendment which reported in 1945. The word 'fair' was seen as an improvement on the then current 'correct',[10] partly because it was more easily distinguishable from 'true' and would stress the need for judgment. It is auditors who continue to support the TFV requirement and to make most use of it in practice.

APPENDIX 3.1

Extract from Coopers & Lybrand Manual, 1986/7, Section 101.05

(i) all information materially affecting the view given by the accounts is properly disclosed and is unambiguous;

(ii) a proper balance is achieved between completeness of disclosure and the degree of summarisation that is necessary if the accounts are to be clear and readily interpretable;

   (iii) the information in the accounts should ensure that the conclusions which a reader might draw from it would be justified and consistent with the circumstances of the enterprise's business;

   (iv) the accounts reflect the substance of the underlying transactions and balances and not merely their form; and

   (v) the presentation adopted in the accounts has not been unduly influenced by management's desire to present facts in a favourable or unfavourable light.

There are also specific suggestions about assets, liabilities and results.

APPENDIX 3.2

Responses to closed-ended questions by size of audit firm
(Big Eight shown first, Next Twelve shown in brackets) (Percentages of relevant respondents)

	Yes	Partly	Yes- and-No	No
1. Specific procedures to check TFV	62.5(75)		37.5(25)	
2. Did 1981 Act change procedures for TFV?	25(25)			75(75)
3. Do you distinguish 'true' from 'fair'?	87.5(75)			12.5(25)
4. Has any client wished to depart from a standard to give a TFV?	87.5(66.7)			12.5(33.3)
5. Has the firm persuaded any client to depart from a standard?	25(16.7)			75(83.3)
7. Has any client wished to depart from law to give a TFV?	87.5(58.3)			12.5(41.7)
8. Has the firm persuaded any client to depart from law?	62.5(25)			37.5(75)
9. Does the Act contain obstructions to a TFV?	50(33.3)			50(66.7)
10. Has any client provided more information to give a TFV?	100(91.7)			0(8.3)
11. Have standards changed procedures for TFV?	25(33.3)		25(8.3)	50(58.3)
12. Does the firm rely on directors for TFV?	0(0)	62.5(91.7)	37.5(8.3)	0(0)
13. Does the firm require a letter re TFV from the directors?	37.5(25)			62.5(75)
14. Should the law change to require directors to state TFV?	87.5(58.3)			12.5(41.7)

APPENDIX 3.3

Private and confidential

Questionnaire to Auditors for ICAEW Research Study

NAME OF RESPONDENT ....

NAME OF FIRM..

RESPONDENT'S POSITION IN FIRM ....

DATE QUESTIONNAIRE COMPLETED ....

Note: This questionnaire is intended to relate to large clients.

Questions

1(a) In order to ensure that a client company's financial statements give a true and fair view, does your firm carry out any procedures which are separate from those used to test compliance with the detailed provisions of the Companies Acts and accounting standards?

YES ☐

NO ☐

1(b) If 'Yes', please give details, referring, where possible, to your audit manual.

1(c) If you have no such procedures, please explain why you consider them not to be necessary.

2 Have the detailed formats and valuation rules introduced originally by the Companies Act 1981 led your firm to change any of the procedures established to ensure that a client's annual financial statements give a true and fair view?

YES ☐

NO ☐

If 'Yes', please give details.

3 In deciding whether or not the financial statements of a client are true and fair, do you distinguish between what is 'true' and what is 'fair'?

YES ☐

NO ☐

If 'Yes' please give details.

4 Within the last 5 years, has a client company ever wished to depart from an accounting standard in order to give a true and fair view?

YES ☐

NO ☐

If 'yes', please give details.

5 Within the last 5 years, has your firm ever persuaded a company to depart from an accounting standard in order to give a true and fair view?

YES ☐

NO ☐

If 'Yes', please give details.

6 What does your firm understand by S228(3) of the Companies Act 1985? In particular, which requirements that might affect the accounts fall outside the 'requirements of this Act as to the matters to be included in a company's accounts or in notes'?

continued

APPENDIX 3.3 – *continued*

Please interpret the 'detailed provisions' mentioned in questions 7 and 8 in the context of S228(3).

7　Within the last 5 years, has a client company ever wished to depart from one of the detailed provisions of the Companies Act in order to give a true and fair view?

　　　　　　　　　　　　　　　　　　　　　　　　　YES ☐
　　　　　　　　　　　　　　　　　　　　　　　　　NO ☐

　　If 'Yes', please give details.

8,　Within the last 5 years has your firm ever persuaded a client company to depart from one of the detailed provisions of the Companies Act in order to give a true and fair view?

　　　　　　　　　　　　　　　　　　　　　　　　　YES ☐
　　　　　　　　　　　　　　　　　　　　　　　　　NO ☐

　　If 'Yes', please give details.

9　Does your firm believe that the Companies Act 1985 contains provisions that obstruct directors and auditors in attempts to present fair accounts?

　　　　　　　　　　　　　　　　　　　　　　　　　YES ☐
　　　　　　　　　　　　　　　　　　　　　　　　　NO ☐

10　Within the last 5 years, has a client company ever provided additional information (without changing the numbers in the financial statements) in order to give a true and fair view?

　　　　　　　　　　　　　　　　　　　　　　　　　YES ☐
　　　　　　　　　　　　　　　　　　　　　　　　　NO ☐

　　If 'Yes', (a) please give details, (b) did you have to persuade the clients to do so?

11　Have any of the accounting standards issued since 1971 led your firm to change any of the procedures it uses to test whether a client company's financial statements show a true and fair view?

　　　　　　　　　　　　　　　　　　　　　　　　　YES ☐
　　　　　　　　　　　　　　　　　　　　　　　　　NO ☐

　　If 'Yes', please give details.

12　Does your firm rely on a client's directors to ensure that their accounts give a true and fair view?

　　　　　　　　　　　　　　　　　　　　　　WHOLLY ☐
　　　　　　　　　　　　　　　　　　　　　　PARTLY ☐
　　　　　　　　　　　　　　　　　　　NOT AT ALL ☐

13　Does your firm require companies to provide a statement stating that, in the directors' opinion, the accounts give a true and fair view?

　　　　　　　　　　　　　　　　　　　　　　　　　YES ☐
　　　　　　　　　　　　　　　　　　　　　　　　　NO ☐

14　Would your firm support a change in the law to require directors of companies to annex to the annual accounts a statement signed by them confirming compliance with the requirement to give a true and fair view?

　　　　　　　　　　　　　　　　　　　　　　　　　YES ☐
　　　　　　　　　　　　　　　　　　　　　　　　　NO ☐

NOTES

1 Since the period of our survey the Act has been amended to make it clear that departure need not necessarily be a secondary option to the provision of additional information. The Act no longer specifically refers to an override, and it obliges directors to state whether accounts have been prepared in accordance with applicable accounting standards and to give particulars of any departure therefrom.

2 The firms, in alphabetical order, were: Arthur Andersen; Arthur Young; Binder Hamlyn; Clark Whitehill; Coopers & Lybrand; Deloitte, Haskins & Sells; Ernst & Whinney; Grant Thornton; Hodgson Impey; Kidsons; KPMG Peat Marwick McLintock; Moore Stephens; Moores & Rowland; Neville Russell; Pannell Kerr Forster; Price Waterhouse; Robson Rhodes; Spicer & Oppenheim; Stoy Hayward; and Touche Ross.

3 Of the 575 companies in the top 900 where the auditors were easy to identify in *Who Audits the UK* (Bohdanowicz, 1984), 477 out of the 575 (i.e. 83 per cent) were audited by fourteen large firms of auditors.

4 Technically, of course, the client of the auditors might be seen to be the body of shareholders or the company as an artificial person. However, in the questionnaire and from now on in this paper, 'clients' is used to mean the directors who, as agents of the shareholders, in effect appoint and arrange the remuneration of the auditors.

5 Of course, breaking a detail of the law may be necessary in order to give a TFV. So, serving the TFV may sometimes require the auditors to condone or encourage 'law breakers'.

6 The UK is unusual in its *requirement* for departures from the details of law. Such departures are not permissible in, for example, Germany, France, the USA and Australia.

7 Under s.228 of the original Companies Act 1985, it seemed that directors were required first to give extra information before resorting to a departure from any legal requirements. This problem appears to be absent in the new s.226, as noted in note 1.

8 It may be that the Big Eight auditors answered differently because their clients are different on average. This might have affected the answers to questions 4, 5, 7, 8 and 10.

9 An explanation suggested by one of our respondents in later discussion is that auditors ask directors for so many different confirmations that the latter may well believe that they have been asked for a TFV statement when in fact they have not.

10 Earlier versions in British law had included various combinations of correct, fair, full and true. Although the practice of accounting and auditing may not have changed over time in this respect, an amendment to law does at least suggest that 'fair' was seen as a better description of what good directors and auditors should aim at. For contemporary comment, see *Accountant* (1944).

REFERENCES

Accountant (1944), 'Editorial', 1 July.

Benston, G.J. (1985), 'The market for public accounting services: demand, supply and regulations', *Journal of Accounting and Public Policy*, Spring.

Bohdanowicz, J. (1984), *Who Audits the UK*, Financial Times Business Information, London.

Brindle, I. (1987), 'Off-balance sheet financing', *Financial Reporting 1986–87*, Institute of Chartered Accountants in England and Wales.

Chandler, R. (1983), 'The annual report: spelling out the responsibility', *Accountancy*, September.

Chastney, J.G. (1975), *True and Fair View – History, Meaning and the Impact of the Fourth Directive*, ICAEW, London.

Coopers & Lybrand (1981), *Manual of Auditing*, 3rd edn, Gee, London.

Coopers & Lybrand (1986), *Manual of Auditing*, London.

De Angelo, L.E. (1981), 'Auditor size and audit quality', *Journal of Accounting and Economics*, August.

Dopuch, N. and Simunic, D. (1982), 'Competition in auditing: an assessment', *Fourth Symposium on Auditing Research*, University of Illinois.

Flint, D. (1982), *A True and Fair View in Company Accounts*, Gee & Co for the Institute of Chartered Accountants of Scotland.

Harris, N.G.E. (1987), 'Fairness in financial reporting', *Journal of Applied Philosophy*, vol. 4, no. 1.

Hopkins, L. (1984), *The Audit Report*, Butterworth, London.

Nobes, C.W. (1990), *Accounting Harmonisation in Europe*, Financial Times Management Reports, London, ch. 8.

Nobes, C.W. and Parker, R.H. (1991), '"True and fair": a survey of UK financial directors', *Journal of Business Finance and Accounting*, Spring.

Russell, Neville (1988), *Business Auditing*, London.

Walker, R.G. (1984), *'A True and Fair View' and the Reporting Obligations of Directors and Auditors*, National Companies and Securities Commission, Melbourne.

Wallace, W.A. (1980), *The Economic Role of the Audit in Free and Regulated Markets*, Touche Ross.

Williams, D.W. (1985), 'Legal perspectives on auditing', in Kent, D., Sherer, M. and Turley, S. (eds), *Current Issues in Auditing*, Harper and Row, London.

This paper by R.H. Parker and C.W. Nobes was first published in Accounting and Business Research, *Autumn 1991*.

4 The True and Fair View Requirement

Impact on and of the Fourth Directive

ABSTRACT

The overriding British legal requirement for financial reporting of giving 'a true and fair view' (TFV) has been exported to continental Europe via the European Community's (EC) Fourth Directive on Company Law. This paper considers accounting rules in continental Europe before this process, and traces the gradual acceptance of the predominance of TFV in the drafting of the Directive after UK accession to the EC. The signifiers used in different European languages in the various drafts of the Directive are examined. It is noted that all (eight) other versions contain only one adjective (generally equivalent to 'faithful') rather than true *and* fair. The origins of the Dutch *getrouw*, the French *fidèle*, etc. are looked into. As the Directive evolved, and particularly as it was implemented in the twelve EC states, greater linguistic variety emerged, such that five countries changed the wording from the original Directive and two others qualified the wording. Whether this affects what TFV signifies is investigated. Countries can also be divided into several groups with respect to the effects of having the TFV in law. The extremes appear to be the UK and Germany.

This paper traces the development of the true and fair view requirement in the Fourth Directive, and then the relevant effects of this element of the Directive on the laws and practices in EC member states.

In the context of the UK, Walton (1991) suggests that we should follow Saussure (1919) and distinguish between the signifier and the signified when examining the TFV. The signifiers are the words 'give a true and fair view', whereas the signified is the underlying idea. What is signified by a particular signifier can change. For example, in order to give a TFV it might, over time, become necessary: (i) to disclose transfers from reserves, or (ii) to present consolidated accounts of a holding company, or (iii) to capitalize certain leases, or (iv) to include current value information.

It is suggested here that, when studying the TFV, a third dimension is necessary: the effects. There are particularly two types of effect:

(i) any adjustments (designed to promote a TFV) to detailed account-ing rules at the stage of national implementation of the EC Directives (called here 'direct effects'), and (ii) any continuing effects of the existence of the legal requirement for TFV on directors, auditors and rule-makers (called here 'indirect effects').

This paper examines the signifier in English; in all the other language versions of the EC Fourth Directive; and in the legal implementations in the twelve EC member states. Then there are preliminary observa-tions concerning the signified and the effects throughout the EC.

SOURCE OF TRUE AND FAIR

It will be suggested below that the origins of the concept of the predominance of the 'true and fair view' are British, although the signifiers used in other European languages are, in general, not literal translations of this. The TFV wording (see Table 4.1) appeared first in British law in the Companies Act 1947 and was then consolidated into the 1948 Act (Parker, 1989, pp. 20–1). The previous British legal requirement (e.g. Companies Act 1900, s.23) was that 'a true and correct view' should be given but this was changed after advice from the accountancy profession that 'correct' was too precise a word to reflect the practice of accounting and auditing (Walker, 1984; Rutherford, 1985). Other combinations of 'full', 'fair', 'true' and 'correct' had been used in nineteenth-century laws. The change of signifier in 1947 may have had no effect on what was signified.

The meaning of TFV (what is signified by it) has been discussed elsewhere from several points of view (e.g. Chastney, 1975; Flint, 1982; Rutherford, 1985; Harris, 1987; Lyas, 1992). What is signified by TFV has been acknowledged by lawyers in the UK as changeable because it is related to prevailing accepted accounting practices (Hoffman and Arden, 1983; Arden, 1993). As for effects, it was the absence of rules rather than the presence of the TFV that was traditionally important in the UK. Hopwood (1990) suggests that the TFV became particularly important to Britain only when seen as a means of countering legalism in the 1971 draft of the Fourth Directive. Parker and Nobes (1991) make the related point that the TFV seems to have been increasingly useful to the British profession as accounting rules became more codified in standards (from 1970) and in law (from 1981). The signified and the effects of TFV for British directors and auditors are noted later.

Incidentally, that the same signifier (and similar signifieds) can have different indirect effects (i.e. those not written into the detail of the law) may be illustrated by comparing the UK and Australia.

Table 4.1 General purpose requirements in UK law, German law and the Fourth Directive

1948 Companies Act (s. 149)	1	Every balance sheet of a company shall give a true and fair view of the state of affairs of the company ... and every profit and loss account [etc.].
	3	... the [detailed] requirements of [the 8th Schedule] shall be without prejudice. ... to the general requirements of subsection (1) ...
1965 *Aktiengesetz* (§ 149)	1	The annual financial statements shall conform to proper bookkeeping principles. They shall be clear and well set out and give the surest possible insight of the company's financial position and its operating results pursuant to the valuation provisions.
1971 Draft (Art. 2)	1	The annual accounts shall comprise the balance sheet, the profit and loss account and the notes on the accounts. These documents shall constitute a composite whole.
	2	The annual accounts shall conform to the principles of regular and proper accounting.
	3	They shall be drawn up clearly and, in the context of the provisions regarding the valuation of assets and liabilities and the lay-out of accounts, shall reflect as accurately as possible the company's assets, liabilities, financial position and results.
1974 Draft (Art. 2)	1	(as 1971 Draft)
	2	The annual accounts shall give a true and fair view of the company's assets, liabilities, financial position and results.
	3	They shall be drawn up clearly and in conformity with the provisions of this Directive.
1978 Final (Art. 2)	1	(as 1971 Draft)
	2	They shall be drawn up clearly and in conformity with the provisions of this Directive.
	3	The annual accounts shall give a true and fair view of the company's assets, liabilities, financial position and profit or loss.
	4	Where the application of the provisions of this Directive would not be sufficient to give a true and fair view within the meaning of paragraph 3, additional information must be given.
	5	Where in exceptional cases the application of a provision of this Directive is incompatible with the obligation laid down in paragraph 3, that provision must be departed from in order to give a true and fair view within the meaning of paragraph 3. Any such departure must be disclosed in the notes on the accounts together with an explanation of the reasons for it and a statement of its effect on the assets, liabilities, financial position and profit or loss. The Member States may define the exceptional cases in question and lay down the relevant special rules.

What is signified by TFV in the UK and Australia is probably very similar in terms of how things should be valued and measured and what things should be disclosed (e.g. Parker, 1991a). However, the legal imposition of TFV in Britain is an overriding one (see Table 4.1), but in Australia TFV overrides neither law nor standards. The Australian Corporations Act 1989 (amended 1991) provides only that the directors shall 'add such information and explanation as will give a true and fair view' (s. 299(1)) (Miller, 1993; Parker, 1994). In the US, a different signifier is used, but here the indirect effect is also clearly different from that in the UK: US financial statements are required to 'present fairly *in conformity with* generally accepted accounting principles'.[1]

In summary, in terms of indirect effects, the TFV may be used by standard-setters, directors or auditors in the UK, Australia and the US. However, only in the UK can it also be used to override the law or standards.

For the present purpose, the distinguishing features of TFV in EC Directives are taken as being (i) the implication of an underlying reality, the portrayal of which is more important than any particular rules of practice, and, therefore, (ii) the requirement for the rules to be broken if this is necessary in order to portray the reality.

IMPACT ON THE DIRECTIVE

The work on the *avant projet* for the Fourth Directive began in 1965 under the chairmanship of Dr Elmendorff.[2] Elmendorff's committee, which first met in 1966, comprised professional accounting experts from the six countries that were then members of the EC. It was to be expected that a German would chair such a project, because the Germans had the most developed company law on accounting in the EC, in particular their public companies Act, the *Aktiengesetz* (AktG) of 1965.

German law, in common with the rules of most continental countries, had no explicit or implicit requirement for TFV. The relevant section of the AktG (§ 149) is reprinted in Table 4.1. It requires that a surest possible insight (*einen möglichst sicheren Einblick*) is to be achieved but only as far as is possible in accordance with the valuation provisions of the Act. This implies that overvaluation is not acceptable but that undervaluation is.[3] Clarity is also mentioned but truth and fairness are not. In France, the requirement was *regularité et sincerité*;[4] in Italy, *chiarezza e precisione* and *evidenza e verità*[5] (see Ferrero, 1991 for more details). The main purpose[6] of these words seems not to signify 'fair' in its sense of 'not misleading', and the rules certainly did not require departures from the detail of the regulations on this basis.

The Elmendorff Committee delivered a draft of the Fourth Directive to the EC Commission in 1968 (and a draft of the Seventh in 1970). The Committee last met in 1970. The first draft of the Fourth Directive was published by the Commission in 1971. The general purpose clause (Article 2, paragraphs 2 and 3) bore a strong resemblance to that in the AktG, as Table 4.1 shows. Here, again, fairness did not feature, and 'accuracy' was to be subject to the provisions of the Directive. The requirement to use 'principles of regular and proper accounting' would have been familiar to German lawyers or auditors but not to those of all other EC countries.

January 1973 saw the arrival of the UK, Ireland and Denmark in the Community. Denmark had little accounting law; it had accepted Anglo-American influences since World War II but had no TFV or similar requirement (Christiansen, 1992, p. 104). The UK and Ireland also had little law on how to do accounting, but they did have the legal predominance of 'true and fair'. Negotiation led to many changes in the Directive, some of which are discussed by Nobes (1983). In particular, as Table 4.1 shows, the TFV requirement was to be found in the second published draft (1974) of the Directive. It has been confirmed[7] by the secretary to the Elmendorff Committee and by the EC Commission that it was the UK's accession to the EC that began this process. The requirement to use principles of regular and proper accounting was changed to a requirement to conform to the provisions of the Directive.

The only continental EC country which was an exception to the lack of TFV was the Netherlands, where the Annual Accounts of Enterprises Act 1970 contained the overriding requirement that accounts should enable a sound insight and should be shown faithfully and systematically (see Table 4.2 and Appendix 4.1). It has been suggested elsewhere that Dutch accounting should be seen as having more in common with Anglo-Saxon than with continental accounting (e.g. Parker, 1991b). The word for 'faithful' (*getrouw*) may also mean fair, as discussed below. It seems that the prior lack of such a provision in Dutch accounting law was due more to the sparseness of law than to any point of philosophy or practice. Although Dutch *accounting* law had no TFV requirement before 1970, the Registeraccountants Act (Auditing Law) of 1962 required the auditor to testify to faithfulness (*getrouwheid*). In accounting and auditing practice, '*getrouw*' also has a long history, as explained in the following section.

The influence of the *Groupe d'Etudes* should be mentioned here. This committee of EC accountancy bodies had been formed at the request of the EC Commission in order to advise on matters such as Directives.[8] The Elmendorff Committee was a predecessor. Representatives

Table 4.2 The origins and spread of true and fair (for translations see Appendix 4.1)

1 Country	2 Words in Law before Directive (first appearance)	3 Words in Directive	4 Implementation of Directive	5 Words in Law if Different from Directive
UK	a true and fair view (1947)	a true and fair view	1981	—
Ireland	a true and fair view (1963)		1986	1. (as in 1970)
Netherlands	1. geeft een zodanig inzicht dat een verantwoord oordeel kan worden gevormd ... 2. geeft getrouw en stelselmatig (1970)	een getrouw beeld	1983	2. geeft getrouw, duidelijk en stelselmatig et retvisende billede
Denmark	—	et pålideligt billede	1981	—
France	—	une image fidèle (een getrouw beeld in Flemish)	1983	—
Luxembourg			1984	—
Belgium			1985	
Germany	—	ein den tatsächlichen Verhältnissen entsprechendes Bild	1985	Unter Beachtung der Grundsätze ordnungs- mässiger Buchführung (then, as Directive)
Greece	—	ten pragmatiki ikona	1986	—
Spain	—	una imagen fiel	1989	la imagen fiel ... de conformidad con las disposiciones legales
Portugal	—	uma imagem fiel	1989	uma imagem verdadeira e apropriada (1989 plan)
Italy	—	un quadro fedele	1991	rappresentare in modo veritiero e corretto

from the UK, Ireland and Denmark joined fully when their countries acceded to the EC in 1973. However, before this, the *Groupe d'Etudes* had already come to the view[9] that the TFV was the right accounting philosophy. This may seem curious, but the UK already had observer status at the *Groupe d'Etudes*. Also, although it has been sometimes impossible to persuade, for example, the German government to agree with certain Anglo-Saxon accounting ideas, it has been easier to achieve consensus with the German accountancy profession, often represented by partners from German offices of multinational accounting firms.[10] The Economic and Social Committee (ECOSOC) of the EC is required to give opinions on draft Directives. In February 1973, it suggested that 'faithful picture' should replace 'accuracy' in Article 2.3 of the 1970 draft. However, the *Groupe d'Etudes* and the ECOSOC did not propose the predominance of TFV over rules.

The 1974 draft of the Directive contained requirements both to give a TFV and to comply with the provisions of the Directive. However, the draft did not deal with cases where the two requirements might conflict. One interpretation of this is that use of the provisions would automatically lead to a TFV, so that the specific TFV requirement related to matters on which there were no provisions or to cases where there was a need to give extra information. As will be explained, this is the German view, and by implication, it is also now the view in the US and Australia, as already noted. This interpretation was not acceptable to the profession in countries like the UK, where it is argued that the TFV is the ultimate objective, which implies the need in certain circumstances to override other legal provisions (e.g. Tweedie, 1983). For example, from this standpoint, the practice in some continental countries of writing off assets for accounting purposes in order to take advantage of generous tax depreciation might be legally sanctioned but should not be permitted in accounts because it would not give a true and fair view.

This full-blooded version of the significance of TFV (discussed further later) triumphed in the adopted version of the Directive in 1978, as shown in Table 4.1. At the formal level, this could be seen as a victory for Anglo-Saxon accounting philosophy. Its effects on practice are more complex, as will be seen later.

LANGUAGE IN THE DIRECTIVE

Rutherford (1983) sets out the signifiers analogous to TFV in the versions of the Directive in six languages. Table 4.2 (column 3) in this paper shows the signifiers in all the languages as prepared by the EC

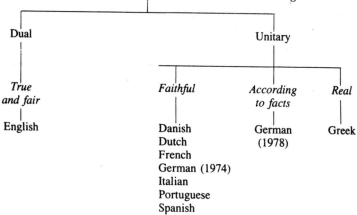

Figure 4.1 'True and fair' signifiers in the Fourth Directive

Commission in the adopted Directive of 1978 (and subsequently for Greece, Spain and Portugal). It seems possible to classify these as in Figure 4.1, using literal translations of the adjectives involved. On this basis, eight[11] languages have a unitary wording and only English has a dual wording (i.e. true *and* fair).

Whether the English 'true and fair' signifies a dual concept or a portmanteau is investigated elsewhere by Walker (1984), Nobes and Parker (1991a) and Parker and Nobes (1991). These last two papers conclude that UK financial directors of large companies see TFV as unitary. However, their auditors see it as dual: approximately, 'truth' is taken to mean that the accounts are in accordance with facts, and 'fairness' that they are not misleading.

What is the origin of the unitary signifier? Column 2 of Table 4.2 shows any analogous wording in laws before the Fourth Directive. It has been suggested above that only the UK, Ireland and the Netherlands had 'true and fair' or its analogue. Given that all the other versions use a unitary signifier, can it be maintained that English is the source? As shown in the next paragraph, it seems that Britain is the main source of the idea that there is an underlying TFV, the presentation of which should override rules. However, we need to look elsewhere for the source of the predominant type of signifier.

Given (i) that, even in the Netherlands, earlier law did not actually refer to the '*getrouw beeld*' of the Directive, (ii) that the draft Fourth Directive had no TFV requirement until *after* the UK and Ireland had joined the EC, and (iii) the confirmation from the Elmendorff Committee, the case for British origins of the idea seems certain. Parker (1989) certainly regards the TFV as a British export to the Commonwealth and then the EC. The Spanish also acknowledge a British origin (Socías, 1991, p. 38), as do the Germans (Busse von Colbe, 1984, p. 121) and the French (CNCC, 1984). Further, as will be noted later, the Italian Ministerial Commentary on their 1991 law specifically refers to the British version as the original. Nevertheless, Ordelheide (1993) points out that the exact formulation of the Fourth Directive was an EC matter, and that the resulting TFV sections in all EC laws sweep away previous provisions, including the British. In particular, all official language versions are formally equal, and none is to be seen as the original.

Given the clear British origins of the overriding nature of the TFV, the source of the majority unitary signifier needs to be investigated in more detail. The Dutch word '*getrouw*' had been evident outside the law before the Auditing Act of 1962 and the Accounting Act of 1970. Its origins have been traced back to the audit report of Cooper Brothers Co. and Price, Waterhouse & Co. in the 1932 annual report of Unilever (Zeff *et al.*, 1992, p. 99). The original English version of the audit report said 'true and correct view'; the Dutch translation was '*getrouw beeld*', which it remained even when the British Companies Act 1947 caused the English version to change to 'true and fair view'. This seems reasonable, as it has already been suggested that, although the English signifier changed in 1947, there was no intention to change what was signified. Not only was '*getrouw beeld*' seen as the best translation of the two different English phrases, but also of the American 'present fairly' (Zeff *et al.*, 1992, p. 101). However, as noted earlier, the US 'present fairly' has a noticeably different significance from the British 'give a true and fair view', and Zeff (1990) argues elsewhere that the best English signifier for the Dutch '*getrouw beeld*' is given by the British phrase not the American.

The French signifier '*image fidèle*', which has a clear echo in the later Italian '*quadro fedele*' or Spanish '*imagen fiel*', can be traced back in the accounting literature to 1920 (Chaveneau, 1920). It seems that a draft French law of 1921 would have required balance sheets to give '*une image aussi fidèle que possible*' (Pasqualini, 1992, p. 37). The word '*fidèle*' in this context can be traced back further to a law in Berne of 1860 and the Swiss Commercial Code of 1863 (ibid., p. 37).[12] It seems that this French expression was 'the leading one' in the Commission.[13] The unitary wording '*fidèle*', like any other adjective, has layers of meaning. At one level, it could imply 'faithful' as in 'faithful representation' (e.g. IASC's Conceptual Framework, para. 33). At another level, it could signify preparation of the accounts 'in good faith'. However, the French governmental body in charge of the *plan comptable* suggested that '*image fidèle*' was a bad translation of TFV, without offering an alternative (CNCC, 1984).

The German signifier in the 1974 draft of the Directive fitted neatly with all these continental equivalents (i.e. *einen getreuen Einblick*). '*Einblick*' had been the word in the 1965 AktG. However, the final version of the Directive moves away from both adjective and noun to '*ein den tatsächlichen Verhältnissen entsprechendes Bild*' (see Appendix 1 for translation). Incidentally, in all other languages the Directive's signifiers for TFV in 1978 are the same as those in 1974.

It is clear that the use of a unitary signifier tells us little about what is signified. This will be examined further in the later section on language in the EC laws.

A Note on Language in the Seventh Directive

The Seventh Directive concerns consolidated accounts. As noted above, an early draft was prepared by the Elmendorff Committee in 1970, but a draft was not published by the Commission until 1976 nor adopted by the Council until 1983. The Seventh Directive applies many of the provisions of the Fourth to group accounts and specifically demands that, 'Consolidated accounts shall give a true and fair view of the assets, liabilities, financial position and profit or loss of the undertakings included therein taken as a whole' (Article 16(3)). The rest of Article 16 contains the overriding TFV provisions as in Article 2 of the Fourth Directive (see Table 4.1).

The Seventh Directive uses the same signifiers in all languages for TFV as the Fourth Directive had done. For example, despite the fact that Denmark had before 1983 already implemented signifiers different from the Danish version of the Fourth Directive (see next section, and Table 4.2), the Danish version of the Seventh Directive uses the same signifiers as the Fourth. One interesting point is that the 1976 German draft of the Seventh Directive used the '*einen getreuen Einblick*' wording (as in the 1974 draft of the Fourth Directive), whereas the 1978 draft and the 1983 final versions used the longer wording of the 1978 final version of the Fourth Directive (see Table 4.2).

IMPACT OF THE DIRECTIVE

The Fourth Directive took many years to implement, as Table 4.2 (column 4) shows. Some countries anticipated the content and then made subsequent legal adjustments (such as Belgium); others were quick off the mark (such as the relative newcomers, Denmark and the UK); some were slow (such as founder EC member, Italy) or had joined the EC after the adoption of the Directive (Greece, Spain and Portugal). The laws come into force on dates after those shown in Table 4.2. In the case of the last country, Italy, this means usually implementation for 31.12.1993 year ends. The more general effects of the Fourth Directive are examined elsewhere (e.g. Gray and Coenenberg, 1984). This paper examines the TFV specifically.

The implementation of the TFV requirement shows the ability of countries to impose their own culture on what, to some of them, was an alien concept. This expresses itself in the signifiers, the signified and the effects.

Signifiers and the Signified

When it comes to implementation of the laws in the member states, several further linguistic complications are added to those of the previous section, as column 5 of Table 4.2 shows. In seven cases (for the five exceptions, see below), the national laws implementing the Directive follow the words in the Directive as prepared in Brussels. The Belgian law implements both the French and the Dutch signifiers from the Directive. The Luxembourg law implements the French. The lengthy wording in the German law follows from the Directive as adopted in Brussels rather than being a subsequent invention of the German parliament. However, as discussed later, even in the German case (and the Spanish) important words were *added*.

The five departures from the Directive's signifiers will now be examined. The Dutch revised earlier legal wordings rather than exactly following the Directive. The 1970 Law was amended by adding the word '*duidelijk*' (clearly) from Art. 2.2 of the Directive. Other national implementations also contain the clarity requirement. The Dutch also retained the fundamental requirement of giving a sound insight, and it is this requirement which is the overriding one. The Danes substituted '*retvisende*' for the Directive's '*pålideligt*', moving from 'faithful' towards 'right-looking' or 'not misleading', which seems close to 'fair'.

In the case of Italian, the Directive used the word '*fedele*' (consistent with the Dutch/French), but this was rejected by the drafters of the Italian law. The train of linguistic events is somewhat complex. The 1942 Civil Code allows departure from the legal valuation rules for *speciali ragioni* (special reasons).[14] This ambiguous provision did not lead in practice to major departures, even for inflation accounting in the 1970s. However, in the revaluation law of 1983 (so-called Visentini-bis;

72/1983, Art. 9), *speciali ragioni* were defined as those where departure from legal rules was necessary in order to give *un quadro fedele*. As mentioned earlier, these Italian words had first appeared in published form in Article 2 of the draft EC Directive in 1974.

When it came to the drafting of the Italian law to implement the Fourth Directive (Decreto Legislativo n. 127/1991), the words '*quadro fedele*' were deliberately not used, perhaps because they already had the above particular usage in Italian law. In the *Relazione Ministeriale* (Ministerial Commentary) to the new law, it was stated that '*rappresentare in modo veritiero e corretto*' had been adopted because '*sembra costituire la più esatta traduzione dell'espressione* true and fair view *dalla quale trae origine la norma della Direttiva*'.[15]

Despite this attempt to match the English, '*veritiero e corretto*' seems nearer to the abandoned British phrase 'true and correct' (although it has already been noted that the Dutch translation of 'true and fair' was the same as that for 'true and correct'). The word '*corretto*', in a law in a Roman law country, appears to mean[16] 'in accordance with legal rules'. The Ministerial Commentary states that '*veritiero*' requires that the preparers of the accounts '*operino correttamente le stime*' (make correct valuation estimates); so '*veritiero*' rests partially on '*corretto*'. In combination, '*veritiero e corretto*' does not seem intended to signify what is understood in the UK by 'true and fair'.

The Spanish moved from 'a faithful picture' to 'the faithful picture' as discussed below. The *Plan General de Contabilidad*[17] notes that *la imagen fiel* deals with the double concept of lack of bias and objectivity, and there is also a reference to truth.[18] The Portuguese have the Directive's '*imagem fiel*' in the Commercial Code but departed from this in the *Plano Oficial de Contabilidade* in an attempt to translate the English original. The resulting '*verdadeira e apropriada*' seems the most literal of all the versions.

In terms of a classification of the signifiers in laws, four out of twelve countries have a dual expression, as shown in Figure 4.2. However, this superficial classification disguises the fact that:

1 a dual signifier can have a more unitary meaning (e.g. in Italy, '*veritiero*' is defined partly in terms of '*correttamente*'), and by contrast

2 a single adjective (e.g. *fidèle* or *fiel*) can have layers of meaning.

There is a further linguistic point. In most translations, the indefinite article is used, leading to the conclusion (e.g. Flint, 1982; *Mémento Pratique Francis Lefebvre*, 1992, 355, 3, 3) that a number

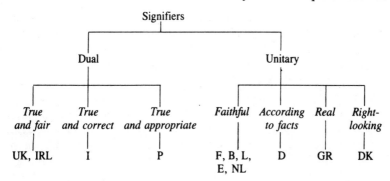

Figure 4.2 'True and fair' signifiers in national rules

of different financial statements could give *a* true and fair view of any particular state of affairs or profit or loss.

The exceptions are:

1 *Italian Law.*Although the Italian Directive had '*un quadro fedele*', the law rephrases the requirement in such a way that no article is used.
2 *Spanish Law.* Although the Spanish Directive had '*una imagen fiel*', the Spanish Law substitutes '*la imagen fiel*', which is also followed in audit reports.[19] It has been suggested that this is an attempt to imply precision in the law.[20]
3 *Dutch Law.* As Table 4.2 shows, the law departs from the Directive in a way that avoids using an article.
4 *Greek Directive and Law.* In Greek, *the* real picture is to be presented. This may have appeared to the Greek draftsmen to make linguistic sense because, although there could be several reasonable/faithful pictures, it might have been thought that there can only be one *real* picture (however philosophically unsound that might be).

Conclusion on What is Signified

The section immediately above has to some extent considered what is signified by TFV. It seems clear that, although changes in rules and practice affect TFV, it must be intended to have an existence independent of rules or general practice. Otherwise, the Fourth Directive's requirements in Article 2.4 and 2.5 for extra information or departure from rules would not make sense. A further example is Article 14 of the Seventh Directive, which requires exclusion of dissimilar subsidiaries from consolidation when inclusion would not give a TFV.

Ordelheide (1993) suggests that, in cases of conflict, the ultimate meaning of TFV in any (or all) EC jurisdictions can now only be decided by the European Court, which may construe a meaning quite different from that intended by the inventors of the source phrase. One can certainly agree with Ordelheide that the UK meaning may not be legally relevant elsewhere. However, given that what is signified by TFV is related to practice (i.e. to what the readers of accounts expect to see), and given that practice is clearly different in different EC countries, it is hard to see that a Court could arrive at the view that TFV meant the same thing in each EC country. Bird (1984) concurs that different signifieds are likely to arise, as does Van Hulle (1993). Ordelheide has suggested[21] that, in practice, the Court would set out a broad enough meaning that different countries could fit their different interpretations into it. Van Hulle (1993) also provides a gloss on this by suggesting that, even though accounts may give a TFV in their state of origin:

> in order to be true and fair for readers in another Member State, some further explanations are no doubt required. This is the reason why the Accounting Directives require in many instances further information in the notes to the Accounts.

However, it seems implausible that a Danish company could be taken to task for not making disclosures that might specifically help a Greek reader. Presumably, also, Van Hulle did not intend the apparent implication that this was the only or the main reason for further disclosures.

Effects

As noted earlier, it seems possible to distinguish between (i) any direct effects on detailed accounting rules that may have accompanied the implementation of the TFV, and (ii) the continuing indirect effects of the legal imposition of the TFV requirement. With respect to the overriding nature of the TFV, the idea that departure from a specific provision of the law should rest upon the opinion of standard-setters, directors or auditors is hard to accept, even for English lawyers (Tweedie and Kellas, 1987), let alone for those in a civil law framework. The national stances towards the implementation of the Directive may be classified into three main types:

(i) *Continued dominance of TFV.* In the UK and Ireland, the continued primacy of the TFV has been used both by standard-setters and by directors and auditors to enable commerecial circumstances of various sorts to prevail over specific legal considerations (Parker and Nobes,

1991). The primacy of TVF has been used by the standard-setters to override the details of the law in several cases. For example:

1 SSAP 9 (Stocks and Work in Progress, para. 39 and Appendix 3, para. 12) suggests that LIFO should not normally be used because it will not give a true and fair view, whereas the Fourth Directive (Art. 40) and the British law specifically allow it (Companies Act 1985, Schedule 4).
2 SSAP 19 (Investment Properties) requires investment buildings not to be depreciated whereas the Fourth Directive and, therefore, the British law require all fixed assets with limited useful lives to be depreciated (Companies Act 1985, Schedule 4).
3 Other cases where 'true and fair' has been used may not override the detail of the law but address conflicts in it. For example, SSAP 20 (Foreign Currency Translation) requires the taking to income of gains on unsettled long-term foreign currency loans. This is not 'prudent', which is a mandatory principle in the Directive, and therefore the gains are not distributable. However, the Directive (Article 31.2) and the British law do allow departures from the basic principles for accounting. SSAP 20 claims that, in this case, the accruals convention (also a mandatory principle in the Directive) should override prudence in order to give a TFV.

The EC Contact Committee has concluded that the TFV override can only be used in cases relating to individual companies rather than to general circumstances (EC, 1990). This would be a problem for the UK at least for point 2 above.[22] However, the conclusions of the Contact Committee have no direct authority, and Alexander (1993) suggests that the Committee's conclusion is clearly invalid in terms of the Fourth Directive, given that Article 2.5 allows member states to define the exceptional circumstances and lay down the relevant special rules. This seems correct, despite Van Hulle's (1993) suggestion that Article 2.5 was designed to restrict flexibility not to increase it. To take the UK as illustration, according to the British Companies Act 1985 (as amended in 1989), the Accounting Standards Board can be interpreted as being delegated with the setting of accounting standards on behalf of the member state, so a standard could define departures for the member state (though only for exceptional cases).

A further aspect of the indirect effects of TFV concerns whether departure from legal provisions is to be seen as a last resort to be used only when even extra information is insufficient. This seems to be the view of the Contact Committee (EC, 1990). However, it is not the view of UK standard setters (e.g. Tweedie and Kellas, 1987, p. 93). The

Companies Act 1989 amended the TFV section to move the law more towards the standard setters' view.[23]

Cases where UK directors have not complied with law in the name of TFV include, for example, non-consolidation of subsidiaries or departure from formats of financial statements. Cases of non-compliance with standards include the base stock method of inventory valuation and non-revaluation of investment properties (Parker and Nobes, 1991, p. 355).

In the Netherlands, the primacy of 'sound insight' and 'faithful' also continues (see Table 4.2). These concepts are used by the *Raad voor de Jaarverslaggeving* (RJ, Council for Annual Reporting; see Parker, 1991b or Zeff et al., 1992) when producing *Richtlijnen* (Guidelines), and by directors and auditors when interpreting the law and Guidelines or in areas where there is no such guidance. However, since the Netherlands has a Civil Code system, the RJ would not feel able to set Guidelines which overrode law. Countries other than the UK and Ireland interpret the 'special circumstances' of Article 2.5 of the Directive (see Table 4.1) in a way that would not allow general departures to be formulated.

(ii) *Enthusiastic change.* In some countries, the implementation of the Fourth Directive was used as a means of changing accounting in an implicitly Anglo-Saxon direction. Governments (including stock-market regulators) may have already been moving in this direction as capital markets expanded and international capital flows grew. Denmark, for example, was first to implement the Directive, included many options and seems closer in line with the UK and the Netherlands now than before the Directive. In the case of France, it has been suggested that the *image fidèle* requirement had the direct effect of undermining the strength of tax-based rules (Pham, 1984), though the relationship between tax and accounting is complex (Standish, 1991). The undermining is only obvious in the regulations relating to consolidated accounts (where tax is not relevant) which result from the implementation of the Seventh Directive. Moves in the direction of Anglo-Saxon accounting had already been made by many large French groups, and such a process suited the Stock Exchange regulatory body, the Commission des Opérations de Bourse. Article 29 of the Seventh Directive is relevant here. It allows that:

> a member state may require or permit the use in the consolidated accounts of other methods of valuation [than the parent's] in accordance with the [Fourth Directive].
>
> (Article 29.2)

Where assets to be included in consolidated accounts have been the subject of exceptional value adjustments solely for tax purposes, they shall be incorporated in the consolidated accounts only after those adjustments have been eliminated. A member state may, however, require or permit [no] elimination, . . . provided [disclosure].

(Article 29.5)

No member states have *required* the 'other methods' of Article 29.2, but all except Portugal and Greece have allowed them. In no member state is there a requirement not to permit the eliminations of Article 29.5. The result of this combination of provisions is that companies in most member states have greater room for manoeuvre in group accounts than in individual accounts.

In the case of France, group accounts can move, and for many groups have moved, away from former tax-based rules towards several 'substance over form' and accruals accounting features, such as the capitalization of leases, the recognition of deferred taxation, and the recognition of unsettled gains on currency amounts (Scheid and Walton, 1992).

The authoritative *Mémento Pratique Francis Lefebvre* (1992) suggests that the effects in France of the legal requirement to give *une image fidèle* should be in those areas where the rules do not exist or where they are not sufficiently detailed. A further point is that the French implementation of the Directive's Article 2.4 (see Table 4.1) requires the extra information to be given '*dans l'annexe*' (in the Notes), whereas the Directive and, for example, the UK law do not specify where, allowing for the financial statements themselves to contain the extra information.

To some extent, the moves away from tax-based and legal form accounting are reflected in Spain. Indeed, it has been suggested that the arrival of the TFV led to a 'thorough accounting transformation' (Casanovas, 1992). One specific example is that substance over form has been addressed in the area of leasing. The 1989 law implementing the Fourth Directive requires finance leases to be capitalized. However, because this might appear to be 'untrue' in law even if 'fair' in substance, the 1990 *Plan General de Contabilidad* requires the leases capitalized to be shown as intangible assets (i.e. the *rights* to use the assets), whereas in other capitalizing countries they would be included as tangible assets.

Despite some changes, Spain has nevertheless put *imagen fiel* firmly into the context of legal provisions. The Commercial Code (book 1, ch. III, section 2, art. 34,2) states: 'The annual accounts must be drafted with clarity and show the true and fair view of the net assets, financial situation and net profit or loss of the business, in conformity with the legal provisions.' The last five words are not in the Directive, nor in the laws of most member states[24] (see the further German exception below). The 1990 *Plan General de Contabilidad* also states (part 1, Accounting Principles, para. 1) that:

> The application of the accounting principles included in the following sections should mean that annual accounts, drafted with clarity, will show the true and fair view of the net assets, financial situation and net profit or loss of the business.

This makes it even clearer in Spain than in France that, although the TFV seems to have affected specific rules, this does not imply that individual companies and auditors have much freedom to apply it.

In Portugal, too, the implementation of the Fourth Directive saw the official *Comissão de Normalização Contabilística* using words in the plan (see Table 4.2) that were designed[25] to establish a legal basis to allow movement away from tax rules in certain cases. The plan also requires substance over form (Principle 4f). The combination of these requirements has led to uncertainty in Portugal, for example about the need and legality of revaluations in times of price instability (Fernandes Ferreira, 1992).

The FEE Survey of published accounts shows (from a fairly small sample)[26] the following on the subject of departures from legal provisons in order to give a true and fair view:

> In 10 instances departures from provisions of the national legislation for that reason are reported: in Belgium, Denmark (three), France (two), Ireland, Luxembourg (two) and the United Kingdom. In seven of those 10 cases the reason for the departure was explained in the accounts.

> (FEE, 1991, p. 27)

FEE (1992) examines this in more detail, showing that the UK and Irish departures were caused by compliance with standards, and three of the other five were departures from formats. It should be noted that a German example does not appear. For Spain, Italy and Portugal, the Directive was not in force for the accounts surveyed.

(iii) *Specific rules continue to override general rules.* In Germany, which seems to be an extreme example of this case, it is assumed that compliance with the legal provisions will normally ensure that a TFV is given.[27] In particular, the *Bilanzrichtlinien-Gesetz* of 1985, which implemented the Fourth, Seventh and Eighth Directives, is the only EC implementation which does not specifically require the true and fair view to override legal provisions in exceptional cases (i.e. it does not implement Article 2.5; see Table 4.1). Further, the German law uses the words from the Directive but, like the Spanish, precedes them with words which might be translated approximately as 'in compliance with accepted accounting principles' (see Table 4.2). This helps to rob the TFV of its significance. There are some legal requirements which have been seen as inimical to TFV (Von Wysocki, 1984). There are even legal views (cited by Ordelheide, 1990, p. 8) that the TFV refers only to the notes to the accounts, and has no effect in interpreting the detailed rules or for filling gaps in rules relating to the financial statements. Certainly, as in France, the German rules require the extra information called for by Article 2.4 of the Directive to be presented in the notes (*im Anhang*).

It is suggested that German tradition would have had to have been overturned in order to allow TFV to override specific rules (Otte, 1990). Unlike in France, there have been few direct effects caused by German legislators making changes designed to reflect commercial substance. This is not, of course, intended to be a criticism of Germany: like the UK, Germany has found its own way of continuing with its traditions despite the Directive. Ordelheide (1990) suggests that national account-ing rules tend to resist attempts at harmonization.

One feature of German accounting that may be seen as a counter-example is the option (§308, HGB) to depart from certain tax-based rules in the preparation of group accounts. A minority of large German groups take advantage of this (Treuarbeit, 1990).

Italy seems to be a further example within this third category of country. First, unlike the cases of France and Spain, no amendments were made to legal accounting principles in Italy specifically in order to allow 'substance' to override 'form', apart from the compulsory con-tent of the Directives themselves. Certainly, the drafters of *principi contabili*[28] would not expect to be able to override the law. Indeed, the implementation of the Directives may cause accounting practices of some large listed groups to move *away* from a number of 'substance-based' practices, in that previously the accounts of listed companies followed *principi contabili* and IASC standards, which are close to UK/US rules. Second, the Ministerial Commentary on the 1991 Law notes that, although it is not possible to specify the exceptional circumstances which would require the rules to be departed from, these would be '*casi veramente eccezionali*'. This suggests extreme rarity or, in practice, that '*veritiero e corretto*' is the same as being in conformity with the rules. Third, the auditors of listed companies were previously required by Presidential Decree to check that accounts followed correct account-ing principles[29] but these words were removed in 1991.

Nevertheless, the legal amendments of 1991 do require far more information than most Italian companies were giving. Also, it is possible that some reduction in the influence of tax law will arise as a result of the testing of *'veritiero e corretto'* in the courts.

Continuum of effects of TFV

From the above discussion it seems possible to suggest that EC countries can be seen as on a continuum with respect to the effects of the TFV. Starting from the most strong, five different positions may be identified (examples of countries are given):

Case I   TFV is used by directors/auditors in interpreting the law and standards or where there is no law or standard, and sometimes to override the law or standards. TFV can also be used by standard-setters to make rules that override details of the law. (UK, Ireland)

Case II   TFV (and 'insight') is used by directors/auditors as the basic principle in interpreting the law and (non-governmental) guidelines. It can be used by them to override guidelines and, potentially, in exceptional cases, the law. It is also used by guideline-setters to make rules but not to override the law. (The Netherlands)

Case III   The arrival of TFV was used by law-makers to allow some change towards 'substance' rather than 'form'. It may be used by directors/auditors when there are no governmental requirements, or to interpret requirements and, in principle, to override them in exceptional cases. (France, Spain)

Case IV   TFV may be used by directors/auditors to interpret government requirements or in cases where there are no requirements. In very exceptional cases, which in practice will probably not arise, it could be used to depart from the law. (Italy)

Case V   It is unresolved whether TFV relates only to notes or whether it might be usable by directors/auditors to interpret government requirements or in cases where there are no requirements. It is clear, however, that TFV cannot be used to depart from the law. (Germany)

SUMMARY AND CONCLUSION

The legal requirement for annual accounts to give a true and fair view uses different signifiers, implies different signifieds and has different effects from time to time and from place to place. A summary of the

Table 4.3 Summary of some relationships between TFV signifier, signified and effects

1 Same signified but different signifiers (e.g. probably little change in 1947 to what the British law signified despite the wording change from 'true and correct' to 'true and fair').
2 Apparently similar signifiers with different signifieds (e.g. the different signifieds of the apparently similar signifiers in the UK and Portugal or in the Netherlands and Spain).
3 Same signifier but changing signified (e.g. changing signified of TFV in the UK, as lease capitalization became standard practice).
4 Same signifier and similar signified but different indirect effects of having TFV in law (e.g. same words in UK and Australia with similar meaning in terms of acceptable or necessary accounting practices for most transactions, but quite different legal status).
5 Same signifier but changing effect of having TFV in law (e.g. the increasing practical importance of having TFV in British law from 1970 to date).
6 Signifiers intended to be the same by the EC Commission but with different effects (e.g. continuum of decreasing significance of TFV in UK, France, Germany).
7 Same non-English signifier to translate three different English signifiers (e.g. the use by the Dutch of *getrouw beeld* to translate 'true and correct view', 'true and fair view' and 'present fairly').
8 Same English signifier represented at different times by more than one signifier in another language (e.g. German signifiers of 1974 and 1978; and changing Danish, Portuguese and Italian signifiers from Directive to national rules).

diversity of the relationships between signifier, signified and effects is shown in Table 4.3, in each case with examples drawn from this paper.

The non-English signifiers at TFV's first official EC appearance in the 1974 versions of the Directive (or later versions for Greek, Spanish and Portuguese) all involve one adjective only (generally corresponding to 'faithful'). The French and Dutch signifiers have decades of history in the context of accounting. By the time the Directive had been implemented into laws, six out of ten non-English-speaking countries had departed from the Directive's original words, apparently in some cases in an attempt to get closer to the English. Further diversity is likely as the Fourth Directive spreads to the European Economic Area and to Eastern Europe, giving rise to signifiers in Swedish, Finnish, Polish,[30] etc.

The reason why the signified changes over time, and presumably from place to place, is because the TFV is connected to practice, although intended to be an independent concept.

In the UK there was little effect in having TFV in law while there were no detailed laws or even standards. However, as regulation increased from the 1970s, so directors and auditors found TFV useful for special cases. At a similar time, the perceived UK need to counter EC-based regulation of accounting, which also involved rules alien to UK practices, gave prominence to the TFV as an argument to be used by the UK profession and by the UK government in Brussels.

Except in Ireland and the Netherlands, there was no analogy to the overriding British TFV requirements elsewhere in Europe. This position has been maintained in practice by Germany, at least for the content of the financial statements themselves. Other EC countries fall between these two extremes, in some cases with the arrival of the TFV being accompanied by significant changes in the accounting rules in the direction of Anglo-Saxon practices. In particular, in some countries (e.g. France and Spain) it seems to have been used by regulators as a philosophy to accompany reform of the rules. However, although the detailed rules have changed, the continuing indirect effects for directors, auditors and rule-makers of the fact that there is a TFV legal requirement are small in these countries.

In some countries, then, the TFV legal requirement has moved from non-existence to existence without effects; in others from non-existence to existence with small direct effects on rules and marginal indirect effects. Paradoxically, in terms of the usefulness of the TFV legal provision to directors, auditors and non-governmental rule-makers, perhaps the greatest *change* in effects from 1970 to date has been in the UK.

APPENDIX 4.1

Translations of words in Table 4.2 and elsewhere

Netherlands	*geeft een zodanig inzicht dat een verantwoord oordeel kan worden gevormd*	presents an insight such that a well-founded opinion can be formed
	geeft getrouw, duidelijk en stelselmatig	presents faithfully, clearly and consistently (over time)
	een getrouw beeld geven	present a faithful picture
Denmark	*et pålideligt billede*	a faithful picture
	et retvisende billede	a right-looking picture
Germany	*(unter Beachtung der Grundsätze ordnungsmässiger Buchführung) ein den tatsächlichen Verhältnissen entsprechendes Bild*	(in compliance with accepted accounting principles) a picture in accordance with the facts

France	*une image fidèle*	a faithful picture
Greece	*ten pragmatiki ikona*	the real picture
Spain	*una (la) imagen fiel ... (de conformidad con las disposiciones legales)*	a (the) faithful picture ... (in conformity with the legal provisions)
Portugal	*uma imagem fiel*	a loyal view
	uma imagem verdadeira e apropriada	a true and appropriate view
Italy	*un quadro fedele*	a faithful picture
	rappresentare in modo veritiero e corretto	present in a true and correct way

NOTES

1 Emphasis added. See Zeff (1992) for an analysis of this case. David Alexander has pointed out that perhaps unpromulgated GAAP could override promulgated GAAP, but it seems unlikely that the SEC would accept this since the SEC gives 'substantial authoritative support' to the FASB in Accounting Series Release 150 of 1973. Also Statement on Auditing Standards 69 puts fairness into the framework of GAAP. This is despite the AICPA Code of Professional Conduct (Rule 203, Interpretation 203-1) which warns against allowing a literal interpretation of a rule to result in misleading financial statements.

2 Dr Elmendorff was trained as a business economist and then a Wirtschaftsprüfer. He was founder of one of the larger German accountancy firms, now Wollert-Elmendorff Deutsche Industrietreuhand GmbH.

3 That is, in addition to the general international requirement for prudence, and the unusually strong German version of this (e.g. Gray, 1980), the AktG requires not the most accurate or the most fair but the most sure/safe insight.

4 In accordance with the rules and in good faith.

5 Clarity and preciseness; obviousness and truth (Civil Code, Arts. 2423 and 2217).

6 The Tribunale di Milano (23 December 1968) held that it meant mainly giving information to all interested parties.

7 Conversation with Horst Kaminski (1 March 1993), and letter from Karel Van Hulle, Head of Company Law Section of the EC Commission (11 January 1993).

8 At the beginning of 1987, a new body, the *Fédération des Experts Comptables Européens* (FEE), took over this role and that of the *Union Européene des Experts Comptables, Economiques et Financiers* (UEC).

9 Published opinion in June 1972.

10 The author uses first hand accounts or personal experience of over a decade's membership of *Groupe* and FEE committees. His memory is confirmed by the FEE Secretary General (letter from John Hegarty, 19 November 1992), and by Karel Van Hulle of the EC Commission (letter of 11 January 1993).

11 Van Hulle (1993, p. 100) is wrong to state that Portuguese has a dual signifier in the Directive. This is so for the Portuguese law but not for the Portuguese versions of the Directives.

12 I am particularly grateful to Alan Roberts for the historical references in this paragraph.

13 Letter from K. Van Hulle of 11 January 1993, and conversation with H. Kaminski of 1 March 1993.

14 '*Se speciali ragioni richiedono una deroga alle norme di questo articolo, gli ammistratori e il collegio sindacale devono indicare e giustificare le singole deroghe nelle loro relazioni all'assemblea*' (Art. 2425).

15 'It seems to represent the most exact translation of the phrase *true and fair view* from which the original rule in the Directive derives.'

16 I am grateful to several Italian colleagues for help in this area. For an earlier reference confirming this, see Colombo (1977) who says that the correct valuation will follow only if and when there is conformity with the rules of the law (p. 19).

17 General accounting plan of 1990, parts 1, 4 and 5 of which are obligatory for Spanish companies. *La imagen fiel* is dealt with in part 1.

18 '*la doble noción de imparcialidad y objetividad*' and '*un tercero podria formarse sobre "la verdadera"*'' (para. 10).

19 E.g. the audit report of Arthur Andersen on CEPSA's 1991 accounts. Interestingly, the company's English translation of the report refers to '*a true and fair view*'.

20 F. Grau, Company Secretary of CEPSA in Brussels on 3 December 1992.

21 Notes from discussion with Dieter Ordelheide at EIASM Conference in Edinburgh, 18 June 1993.

22 It may not be a problem for point (a) because SSAP 9 is merely narrowing down options allowed by the Directive, nor for point (c) where there is a conflict in the Directive.

23 'If in special circumstances [in the case of any company], compliance with any of those provisions is inconsistent with the requirements to give a true and fair view [even if additional information were provided in accordance with sub-section (4)], the directors shall depart from that provision . . . ' S.226 of the 1985 Act as amended; bracketed parts deleted in 1989.

24 The Luxembourg law of 1984 does not include these words, but the official guidance on audit reports from the Institut des Réviseurs d'Entreprises does.

25 Letter of 9 February 1993 from Sen. Fernandes of the Câmara dos Revisores Oficias de Contas.

26 341 Companies from nine EC countries.

27 A minute of the EC Council states that this may normally be taken to be the case (Council R 1961/78 [ES93] 18 July 1978, No. 2).

28 'Accounting principles' as published by a joint committee of the Italian professional bodies: Dottori Commercialisti and Ragionieri.

29 Decreto Presidente della Repubblica No. 136, 31 March 1975: '*secondo corretti principi contabili*'.

30 A Polish ministerial decree of 15 January 1991 requires a true and fair view in the context of the regulations. The words used are '*rzetelny i jasny obraz*', which seem to be literally translated from English. However, an Act, which has higher authority, was passed in October 1991 requiring correctness and honesty (*prawidlowosc* and *rzetelnosc*), which seems

to be drawn from interwar Polish legislation. I am grateful to Marek Schroeder of Birmingham University for this information.

REFERENCES

Accountancy (1990), 'Doubts about UK practice', November, p. 11.

Alexander, D. (1993), 'A European true and fair view?', *European Accounting Review*, vol. 2, no. 1.

Alexander, D. and Archer, S. (1992), *The European Accounting Guide*, Academic Press.

Bird, P. (1984), 'What is "a true and fair view"?', *Journal of Business Law*, November.

Busse von Colbe, W. (1984), 'A true and fair view: a German perspective', in Gray and Coenenberg (1984).

Casanovas, I. (1992), 'Spain and the process of harmonization with EC accounting regulations', in Gonzalo, J.A., *Accounting in Spain*, Asociación Española de Contabilidad y Administración de Empresas, p. 169.

Chastney, J.G. (1975), *True and Fair View – History, Meaning and the Impact of the Fourth Directive*, Institute of Chartered Accountants in England and Wales.

Chaveneau, J. (1920), 'Les bilans – Etablissement et vérifications aux points de vue commercial, industriel et fiscal', *Librairie Arthur Rousseau*, cited in Haddou, G. 'Fiscalité et Comptabilité; Evolution Législative depuis 1920', *Revue Française de la Comptabilité*, July–August 1991.

Christiansen, M. (1992), 'Denmark' in Alexander and Archer (1992).

CNCC (1984), cited in Rutherford (1989) as *Assises Nationales du Commissariat aux Comptes, Documents du Travail*, Compagnie Nationale des Commissaires aux Comptes.

Colombo, G.E. (1977), 'La disciplina italiana della revisione', *Rivista dei Dottori Commercialisti*, January–February.

EC (1990) *Accounting Harmonisation in the EC. Problems of Applying the Fourth Directive*, Commission; commented on in *Accountancy* (1990).

FEE (1991), *European Survey of Published Accounts*, Routledge.

FEE (1992), *Analysis of European Accounting and Disclosure Practices*, Routledge.

Fernandes Ferreira, R. (1992), 'Free valuations of tangible fixed assets', paper presented at the EAA Conference, Madrid.

Ferrero, G. (1991), *I Complementari principi della 'Chiarezza', della 'Verita' e della 'Correttezza' nella Redazione del Bilancio d'Esercizio*, Giuffrè Editore.

Flint, D. (1982), *A True and Fair View in Company Accounts*, Institute of Chartered Accountants of Scotland.

Gray, S.J. (1980), 'The impact of international accounting differences from a security-analysis perspective: some European evidence', *Journal of Accounting Research*, Spring.

Gray, S.J. and Coenenberg, A.G. (1984), *EEC Accounting Harmonization*, North Holland.

Harris, N.G.E. (1987), 'Fairness in financial reporting', *Journal of Applied Philosophy*, vol. 4, no. 1.

Hoffman, L. and Arden, M. (1983), 'Counsel's opinion on true and fair', *Accountancy*, November.

Hopwood, A.G. (1990), 'Ambiguity, knowledge and territorial claims: some observations on the doctrine of substance over form: a review essay', *British Accounting Review*, March, p. 84.

Lyas, C. (1992), 'Accounting and language', in Mumford, M. and Peasnell, K.V. (eds), *Philosophical Perspectives on Accounting*, Routledge.

Miller, M.C. (1993), 'Financial reporting in Australia', in Cooke, T.E. and Parker, R.H. (eds), *Financial Reporting in the West Pacific Rim*, Routledge.

Nobes, C.W. (1983), 'The origins of the harmonising provisions of the 1980 and 1981 Companies Acts', *Accounting and Business Research*, Winter.

Nobes, C.W. (1989), *Interpreting European Financial Statements*, Butterworths.

Nobes, C.W. and Parker, R.H. (1991a), 'True and fair: a survey of UK financial directors', *Journal of Business Finance and Accounting*, Spring.

Nobes, C.W. and Parker, R.H. (1991b) *Comparative International Accounting*, Prentice Hall.

Nobes, C.W. and Zambon, S. (1991), 'Piano, piano: Italy implements the directives', *Accountancy*, July.

Ordelheide, D. (1990), 'Soft-transformations of accounting rules of the Fourth Directive in Germany', *Les Cahiers internationaux de la Comptabilité*, Editions Comptables Malesherbes.

Ordelheide, D. (1993), 'True and fair view – a European and a German perspective', *European Accounting Review*, vol. 2, no. 1.

Otte, H.H. (1990), 'Harmonisierte Europäische Rechnungslegung', *Zeitschrift für Betriebswirtschaft*, no. 42.

Parker, R.H. (1989) 'Importing and exporting accounting: the British experience', in Hopwood, A.G. (ed.), *International Pressures for Accounting Change*, Prentice Hall.

Parker, R.H. (1991a), 'Financial reporting in the UK and Australia', ch. 7 in Nobes and Parker (1991b).

Parker, R.H. (1991b), 'Financial reporting in the Netherlands', ch. 10 in Nobes and Parker (1991b).

Parker, R.H. (1994), 'Debating true and fair in Australia: an exercise in deharmonization?', *Journal of Accounting, Auditing and Taxation*, forthcoming.

Parker, R.H. and Nobes, C.W. (1991), 'Auditors' view of true and fair', *Accounting and Business Research*, Autumn.

Pasqualini, F. (1992), *Le Principe de l'Image Fidèle en Droit Comptable*, Litec.

Pham, D. (1984), 'France' in Gray and Coenenberg (1984).

Rutherford, B.A. (1983), 'Spoilt beauty: the true and fair view doctrine in translation', *AUTA Review*, Spring.

Rutherford, B.A. (1985), 'The true and fair view doctrine: a search for explication', *Journal of Business Finance and Accounting*, vol. 12, no. 4.

Rutherford, B.A. (1989), 'The true and fair doctrine: some recent developments', in Macdonald, G. and Rutherford, B.A., *Accounts, Accounting and Accountability*, Van Nostrand.

Saussure, F. de (1919), *Cours de Linguistique Générale*, Payot: Lausanne, translated as *Course in General Linguistics*, Philosophical Library: New York, 1959.

Scheid, J.C. and P. Walton (1992), 'France' in Alexander and Archer (1992).

Socías, A. (1991), *La Normalización Contable en el Reino Unido, Francia, Alemania y España*, Asociación Española de Contabilidad y Administración de Empresas.

Standish, P.E.M. (1991), 'Financial reporting in France', ch. 8 in Nobes and Parker (1991b).

Treuarbeit (1990), *Konzernabschlüsse '89*, IDW-Verlag.

Tweedie, D.P. (1983), 'True and fair rules', *Accountant's Magazine*, November.

Tweedie, D.P. and J. Kellas (1987), 'Off-balance sheet financing', *Accountancy*, April.

Van Hulle, K. (1983), 'Truth and untruth about true and fair', *European Accounting Review*, Vol. 2, No. 1.

Von Wysocki, K. (1984), 'Germany' in Gray and Coenenberg (1984).

Walker, R.G. (1984), *'A True and Fair View' and the Reporting Obligations of Directors and Auditors*, National Companies and Securities Commission, Melbourne.

Walton, P. (1991), *The True and Fair View: A Shifting Concept*, Occasional Research Paper No. 7, Chartered Association of Certified Accountants.

Zeff, S.A. (1990), 'The English language equivalent of Geeft een Getrouw Beeld', *De Accountant*, October 1990.

Zeff, S.A., (1992), 'Arthur Andersen & Co. and the two-part opinion in the auditor's report: 1946–1962', *Contemporary Accounting Research*.

Zeff, S.A., van der Wel, F. and Camfferman, K. (1992), *Company Financial Reporting: A Historical and Comparative Study of the Dutch Regulatory Process*, North Holland.

This paper by Christopher Nobes was first published in Accounting and Business Research, *Winter 1993.*

5 Debating True and Fair in Australia

An Exercise in Deharmonization?

ABSTRACT

In spite of the internationalization of securities markets and the harmonizing activities of the International Accounting Standards Committee and the European Community, it can be argued that company financial reporting in certain countries has been 'deharmonized' in recent decades rather than harmonized. Australia and the UK are possible examples of this. This paper discusses the phenomenon at the conceptual level by considering the reaction of Australian accountants to the explicit true and fair view requirement 'imported' from UK company law by the Australian states from 1955 onwards. The paper also considers the nature of the debate and its participants and the role of the debate in changing Australian legislative requirements in respect of truth and fairness. It seeks explanations for the quite different reactions of the standard-setters in the two countries to an overriding true and fair requirement and argues that these arose largely from the different national environments in which the standard-setters operated from the 1960s onwards.

During the period when UK accountants were actively exporting the concept of 'true and fair' to the other member states of the European Community (Parker, 1989; Nobes, 1993) Australian accountants were debating the necessity for the concept's existence. This debate is of more than local interest for at least three reasons. First, it can be seen as part of a process in which, international accounting standards notwithstanding (both the UK and Australian were founder members in 1973 of the International Accounting Standards Committee), UK and Australian accounting have been 'deharmonized' rather than 'harmonized'. Second, it can be seen as a case study of the impact of the role of public debate on accounting regulation. Third, it can, when contrasted with the British experience, be seen as an example of the importance of 'territorial claims' in accounting standard-setting. All three aspects are looked at in this paper, but with an emphasis on the first.

HARMONIZATION AND DEHARMONIZATION

International harmonization can be defined as a process of increasing the compatibility of accounting concepts, rules and practices between countries by setting bounds to their degree of variation (cf. Nobes and Parker, 1991b, p. 70). Conversely, international 'deharmonization' may be defined as a process of decreasing the compatibility of accounting concepts, rules and practices between countries by removing those bounds.

Deharmonization is less easy to observe than harmonization. There are no committees charged with the task of international deharmonization! There are, however, national legislators and national standard-setting bodies which consciously or unconsciously change laws or standards so as to make them different from those in another country. It is possible, although not necessary, that deharmonization of country X with country Y takes place because X is attempting to harmonize with country Z. Thus, an explanation of the deharmonizing of Australian and UK financial reporting could be that Australia is harmonizing with the USA and the UK is harmonizing with the European Community. As we shall see later, this explanation is too simple but it is a useful starting point.

It takes two (or more) to harmonize (or deharmonize). Thus one way of looking at harmonization and deharmonization is to see them as part of the process by which accounting concepts, rules and practices are 'imported' and 'exported'. Harmonization is furthered when imports are accepted; deharmonization occurs when previously accepted imports are rejected in favour of new imports or of a domestic product. The present paper is concerned with the deharmonization of a concept, but rules and practices can also be deharmonized.

Harmonization is often discussed in terms of the activities of such international organizations as the International Accounting Standards Committee (IASC) and the Commission of the European Community. The success of these bodies depends, however, very much on underlying cultural and economic factors. Harmonization is most likely to take place where countries share a cultural identity, have common economic interests and have governments with the political will to harmonize. Such was largely the case until the mid-twentieth century for Australia and the UK.

HARMONIZATION THROUGH COLONIZATION

Australia was colonized by the British from 1788. Although the Australian colonies merged to form the Commonwealth of Australia as from 1 January 1901, the country remained in many ways an outpost of Britain. For many Australians, the UK was not only the major trading partner and the major source of capital investment, it was also a cultural 'home'.

A crucial turning-point in changing this was the fall of Singapore in 1942 which led the then Australian prime minister, John Curtin, to write: 'Without any inhibitions of any kind I make it quite clear that Australia looks to America, free of any pangs as to our traditional links of kinship with the United Kingdom' (quoted in Alexander, 1972, p. 164). These 'links of kinship' (and of trade and investment) remained, however, very strong. In a UNESCO survey of 'how nations see each other' carried out in 1948, Australians did not regard the UK as a 'foreign country'. Americans were regarded as foreigners but were the foreigners to whom Australians were most friendly (Buchanan and Cantril, 1953, p. 69).

Throughout most of Australia's accounting history, the influence has been one way: Britain has influenced Australian accounting but Australia has not influenced British accounting. The one exception to this is very recent. The Accounting Standards Committee (ASC) and the Accounting Standards Board (ASB) have both been influenced by the IASC's conceptual framework and the contents of this were much influenced by Australian accountants, albeit building on US foundations.

In the nineteenth century the six Australian colonies, as they then were, tended to adopt British company legislation on a selective basis and after a time-lag, although the Victorian Companies Act of 1896, which was influenced by a companies bill proposed by the UK Davey Company Law Amendment Committee of 1895 which did not become law in the UK, and the Victorian Companies Act of 1938, which required group accounts ten years before UK legislation did, were notably innovative. Nevertheless, until the 1960s the Australian states tended to pass company legislation based on UK companies acts and the recommendations of UK company law amendment committees. There were good economic as well as cultural reasons for this. In the words of a Victorian legislator in 1910: 'Investors at Home were shy about investing in a State whose company law they did not understand' (quoted Gibson, 1971, p. 48). Australians were conscious that theirs was a small community and that the British experience, 'even in the varieties of iniquity', was richer and more complete (Moore, 1934, p. 182).

The Australian habit of copying UK legislation ceased in the 1960s. The UK Companies Acts of 1967 onwards have had relatively little effect on Australian legislation. This trend, already established, was strengthened when UK company legislation ceased to be based on the recommendations of Company Law Amendment Committees and became based instead upon directives agreed in Brussels. Australian financial reporting, unlike that of the UK, has not been Europeanized.

Australian accounting is still of recognizably UK descent. As in the UK, and in contrast to the USA, many of the rules of Australian corporate financial reporting are set out in company law. As in the UK, Australian company law:

1 contains a true and fair requirement;
2 supplements this by a list of detailed specific disclosure requirements;
3 prescribes formats for balance sheets and profit and loss accounts; and
4 requires financial statements to be prepared in accordance with applicable accounting standards.

These similarities are to some extent, however, superficial. In contrast to the UK:

1 the Australian standard setters have, as we shall see, come to oppose rather than support the true and fair view requirement;
2 there are very few measurement requirements in companies legislation; and
3 the formats do not greatly resemble the UK formats.

Australia and the UK are also similar in that a substantial body of accounting rules has been generated, both directly and indirectly, by the activities of the professional accountancy bodies. Moreover, both countries, unlike the USA, still benefit (or suffer from) a number of such bodies which compete as well as collaborate. The Australian bodies are the Institute of Chartered Accountants in Australia and the Australian Society of Certified Practising Accountants (formerly the Australian Society of Accountants).

THE COMING OF TRUE AND FAIR

In the 1950s and 1960s the Australian States, starting with Victoria, enacted Companies Acts which contained true and fair view requirements based on those of the UK Companies Act 1948. The text of the relevant clauses of the Uniform Companies Act of 1961 is given in Appendix 5.1. These followed closely the corresponding clauses in the UK Companies Act of 1948, the most important difference being that the

Australian Acts substituted 'without affecting the generality of the foregoing' for 'without prejudice to'. It was generally agreed in both Australia and the UK that, in the event of a conflict between truth and fairness and the detailed requirements of the Schedule, the requirement to give a true and fair view should prevail (e.g. Ryan, 1967, p. 95) but there was no explicit recognition that this might involve departures from the detailed requirements of the Act. Unlike contemporary UK law and practice, the Australian Acts also required a statement by the *directors* (not just the auditors) that the accounts gave a true and fair view. This requirement can be traced back via the Victorian Companies Act of 1896 to a recommendation of the UK Davey Company Law Amendment Committee of 1895.

From 1946 the Institute of Chartered Accountants in Australia (ICAA) had followed the example of the Institute of Chartered Accountants in England and Wales in issuing Recommendations on Accounting Principles. There was debate as to the extent that the wording of the English Institute should be followed. A majority vote in May 1963 came down in favour of what would now be described as 'harmonization', deciding that the General Council of the Australian Institute would 're-issue the recommendations of the English Institute subject to modifications which may seem to be necessary to suit local conditions' (Zeff, 1973, p. 9). In 1963 the ICAA in its replacement recommendation on the 'Presentation of Balance Sheet and Profit and Loss Account' adopted the wording of the English Institute's reference in its Recommendation No. 18 (1958) to a true and fair view. According to the Recommendation (paras. 3 and 4):

A true and fair view implies appropriate classification and grouping of the items [and] also implies the consistent application of generally accepted principles.

The reference to appropriate classification and grouping can be traced back to the opinion of the British practitioner Sir Russell Kettle (a member of the Cohen Committee on Company Law Amendment) that 'A true and fair view implies that all statutory and other essential information is not only available but is presented in a form in which it can be properly and readily appreciated' (Kettle, 1950, p. 117). Both the Australian and the English Recommendations went on to make it clear that generally accepted principles required a 'historical document'. The recommendations clearly assumed the existence of a recognizable body of generally accepted principles that were adequate to produce truth and fairness, but the use of the word 'implies' was ambiguous. Was adherence to generally accepted principles a sufficient or merely a necessary condition for truth and fairness?

WHY DID A DEBATE TAKE PLACE AND WHO TOOK PART?

Most members of a profession prefer to get on with the job rather than debate it. Such debates as there are tend to be on points of technical detail rather than philosophic approaches. Concepts are taken for granted as self-evident. Chastney (1975, pp. 72–3) notes that:

> The words 'true and fair' seem to have collected around them an aura of mystique which is unjustified. It is almost as if they are part of British culture; as if their abandonment would herald the demise of the accounting profession and would geld the normal audit report. Benson [a leading British practitioner giving evidence to the Jenkins Committee, which reported in 1962] says they are engrained in the profession.

These words were echoed in 1986 by the finance director of a leading UK company:

> The true and fair concept is something which is engrained in accountants. I am fairly sure that in all our discussions with the auditors, and we have many, the term 'true and fair' has never once been used. It is a concept that we all hold in common and not a matter for discussion.
>
> (reported by Nobes and Parker, 1991a, p. 360)

Why then did Australian accountants bother to discuss it?

The debate began in the 1960s in response to the numerous company failures of 1961–3, including in particular the collapse of the Reid Murray group. The failure of the group's published financial statements to give a true and fair view was severely criticized by the inspectors appointed to examine the failures. The Reid Murray inspectors (who were lawyers) commented that what 'accounts show depends so much on the assumptions with which the particular accountant who has prepared them has begun and there are many available assumptions, all with some degree of acceptance among accountants'. They went on to state that 'common sense has compelled us to reject a number of the accounting practices used in the group and apparently regarded as acceptable by accountants' (quoted in Stamp, 1964, pp. 4,11).

The UK also suffered from company failures in the 1960s and consequent criticism of accountants and auditors. These led to the creation of the Accounting Standards Steering Committee (later the Accounting Standards Committee) but not to widespread criticism of the truth and fairness requirement. It is perhaps symbolic of the first stage of deharmonization of UK and Australian accounting that, whilst articles on true and fair were rare in the UK in the 1960s and early 1970s, the articles written by Australian accountants during this period (e.g. Horrocks, 1967; Miller, 1969) could with very little change have been published in the British accounting journals. Australian writers were still well acquainted with the British literature but had difficulty in finding UK accountants to cite apart from Edey (1971).

These differences in Australian and UK reactions to accounting crisis may be attributable to three ways in which the Australian accounting environment differed in the 1960s from that in the UK: an increasing awareness of non-UK and, specifically, American accounting practices; the existence in some states (notably New South Wales) of Registrars of Companies who acted in part as accounting regulators; and the growth (earlier by a decade than in the UK) of a lively academic accounting sector.

The debate took place during a period when overseas investment in Australia increasingly originated in the United States rather than the UK. The latter's share of total investment fell from about two-thirds in the 1960s to around a quarter in the 1970s. During the same period the US share rose to 30 per cent, with new US investment greater than new UK investment. At the same time Australian accountancy firms were increasingly linked to the large international accountancy firms which were perceived to be North American rather than British (Gibson and Arnold, 1981). Australian accountants became more aware that the USA did not have an overriding true and fair requirement but that US auditors were required to affirm that the financial statements 'present fairly in conformity with generally accepted accounting principles'.

Whilst the UK provided the original model for the State Registrars of Companies, the UK Registrar made no attempt to examine the accounts submitted to him. This was, however, done by the NSW Registrar, although the Registrar admitted that he 'would not for one moment contemplate a prosecution based on so slippery a concept as truth and fairness' (Ryan, 1967, p. 107).

A striking feature of the debate was the virtual absence as participants of 'practical men', i.e. the directors and auditors required by legislation to sign statements and reports attesting to the truth and fairness of company financial statements. The main participants in the debate have been academics, including lawyers as well as accountants. They were not, however, cloistered 'academic scribblers' (Whittington, 1983) or 'scholar-saints' (Peasnell and Williams, 1986) but academics who have in many instances worked as regulators for federal or state government agencies or involved themselves closely with the standard-setting activities of the accountancy profession. They have written mainly in professional journals or as financial journalists, and have been concerned to argue in favour of certain policies as against others. This literature can plausibly be dubbed a 'market for excuses' (Watts and Zimmerman, 1979) but it was not one in which 'ersatz academics' (Peasnell and Williams, 1986) supplied excuses inconsistent with 'known truth' on the demand of bureaucrats. The bureaucrats (regulators and standard-setters) have often themselves been academics or former academics and they have been perfectly capable of introducing their own excuses into the literature.

Within Australia, therefore, much more than in the UK, there has been a group of academics-cum-regulators who have been ready to challenge the existing legislation and to seek, in a time of crisis, for alternative solutions. Whittington (1983) assigns four functions to accounting theorists:

1 they supply the list of 'excuses' from which the 'practical man' chooses and thus, by failing to supply adequate excuses for all situations, may constrain the ultimate choice of models;
2 by respecting the principles of logical consistency in theory construction they improve the models ultimately adopted;
3 they clarify the assumptions which are necessary for a theory to be logically valid, the assumptions in turn clarifying conflicts of interest because different interest groups will subscribe to different assumptions; and
4 insofar as assumptions are factual, they establish their accuracy by empirical research.

The participants in the Australian debate fulfilled the first function but made little contribution to the other three. In particular, empirical research has been lacking, with the exception of Houghton (1987), an Australian academic writing in a non-Australian research journal who sought to measure empirically the meanings of the true and fair concept held by accountants engaged in public practice, on the one hand, and non-institutional shareholders on the other. His finding that these two groups hold different 'connotative' meanings of the concept seems to have been ignored by other participants in the debate.

THE DEBATE BEGINS

The earliest discussion of the true and fair view requirement in an Australian textbook is to be found in Johnston and Jager's *The Law and Practice of Company Accounting in Australia* (1st edn, 1963). Both had been accounting teachers at the University of Melbourne, Johnston being a New Zealander with a doctorate from a British university whose previous publications included *The Law and Practice of Company Accounting in New Zealand*. Johnston and Jager (1963, p. 312) pointed out that the term 'true and fair' was very indefinite and identified three broad ways of interpreting it: literally; technically, in accordance with 'accounting principles recommended by leading accountancy bodies or followed in best practice'; or technically, in accordance with 'accepted accounting or business practice which may in the extreme mean merely that "somebody had tried it"'. They argued that the UK Cohen Committee on Company Law Amendment (1945) clearly had in mind a technical interpretation but that there was nothing in the Act itself to say that this was the intention of the legislature and that in case of conflict it was by no means certain that the courts would not apply a literal interpretation.

The technical interpretation was supported in 1960 and 1966 by Yorston and Irish, both leading practitioners and textbook writers: 'The words "true and fair" as applied to financial reports mean true and fair from an accounting viewpoint. The financial report may be true for an accounting standard but not necessarily true in fact' (Yorston, 1960, cited in Ryan, 1980, p. 87). 'The words "true and fair" have a technical legal meaning. . . . They do not mean absolute accuracy with one possible right answer like a sum in arithmetic' (Irish, 1966, p. 172).

SUPPLYING THE LIST OF 'EXCUSES'

The Australian writers on true and fair in the late 1960s and early 1970s were unanimous in condemning the inadequacies of company financial reporting as practised in Australia during that period but not unanimous in their proposals for reform. Birkett (1968), an academic accountant writing in a legal journal, argued that the professional accountancy bodies defined truth and fairness in terms of the generally accepted accounting principles that they themselves promulgated, but that these principles were inadequate to give a true and fair view. He did not in his paper, however, attempt to suggest a remedy. Nor did Dyer (1974) (an academic economist writing in a legal journal) who concluded that it was highly questionable whether 'true' in 'true and fair' can be legitimately defined as truth in any of the four traditional theories of truth put forward by philosophers. The proposals of the other participants in the debate, at the risk of some simplification, can be summarized as follows:

1 *The true and fair requirement would be attainable if historical cost accounting were abandoned.* This was the view of Horrocks, an academic accountant, who argued that what were termed accounting principles were 'merely current practices' (Horrocks, 1967, p. 569). His solution was not to abandon the true and fair requirement but to improve those principles by abandoning historical cost accounting and adopting current value accounting.

2 *The true and fair requirement should be abandoned in favour of a statement that the accounts gave a fair presentation of historical cost information prepared in accordance with normal accounting practice plus supplementary current value information.* This was the view of Johnston (1967), who moved back to New Zealand in 1962 but wrote for an Australian as well as a New Zealand audience. After a detailed survey and discussion he concluded that the standard of a true and fair view was 'misunderstood, misleading and unattainable' and that it could not be administered by accountants acting as auditors unless supported by detailed legislative requirements. He did not agree with those critics of orthodox accounting who 'seem to imagine that all that is necessary to show a "true and fair view of the state of affairs" of a company is to include the assets at "current values" (Johnston, 1967, p. 448). He recommended an auditors' report on the following lines:

> the above balance sheet fairly presents a statement of the assets, unexpired costs, liabilities, capital and reserves prepared in accordance with normal accounting practice, and by way of note the estimated current realisable and replacement values (or government valuation) of such items as it is possible to appraise with reasonable accuracy.

> (ibid., p. 452)

The essential part of Johnston's recommendation is very similar to US practice with 'normal accounting practice' substituted for 'generally accepted accounting principles'.

3 *The true and fair requirement should be abandoned. No reference to fairness should be made but simply a statement that the accounts had been prepared in accordance with company law and 'normal accounting practice'.* This was the view of Miller, an Australian academic accountant who argued that it was 'impossible for any balance sheet and profit and loss account, whether based on historical costs or current values, to supply a true and fair view of the state of a company's affairs'. The Companies Act should not be circumvented by restricting the meaning of 'true and fair' to a narrow

technical sense of 'in accordance with recognised accounting principles' (Miller, 1969, p. 169). Miller provided an amended auditor's report similar to Johnston's but omitted any reference to fairness, stating instead that the information in the accounts is 'presented in accordance with the provisions of the Companies Act and normal accounting practice' (ibid., p. 175).

4 *The true and fair requirement should be abandoned and accounting principles should be laid down by law.* This was the view of Baxt, an Australian academic lawyer writing in a New Zealand professional accountancy journal, who provided a detailed legal analysis, and concluded by recommending that accounting principles should be laid down in the Companies Act:

> If the principles are spelt out with clarity and with sufficient flexibility to allow for variation in the special case, then it is submitted that the term 'true and fair view' will become redundant. Before the law moves in to legislate for the accountants it might be both appropriate and beneficial for the profession to draw up its own rules. The law then might be able to adopt these rather than impose a set of rules which the profession would not welcome.
>
> (Baxt, 1968, p.309)

Writing in very similar vein two years later in an Australian law journal, Baxt (1970) claimed that true and fair accounts were 'a legal anachronism'.

5 *The true and fair view requirement should be abandoned in favour of the American formula under which auditors report their opinion that the accounts present fairly the financial position of the company and the result of its operations in conformity with generally accepted accounting principles applied on a basis consistent with that of the preceding period.* This was the recommendation of Heazlewood (1971) and also of what was perhaps the most important early contribution to the debate: that of the then Registrar of Companies in New South Wales (Ryan, 1967). Ryan approached the topic as an Australian lawyer brought up in the tradition of the English common law, looking in detail at English and Scottish case law, the reports of UK Company Law Amendment committees and authoritative British legal textbooks such as Gower and Palmer. Looking first at the ordinary and natural meaning of the phrase 'true and fair' he argued that it must require that the assets of a company should be represented by accounts which corresponded with the value of the assets at the end of the accounting period (Ryan, 1967, p. 97) but after consideration of the wording of the Ninth Schedule concluded that the words

of the Schedule represented an endorsement by the legislature of the historical cost concept and that accountants were justified in preparing accounts in accordance with that concept.

He went on, however, to regret that:

> The legislation is clearly at odds with itself. On the one hand accounts are to give a true and fair view, while on the other we are apparently required to interpret those words in a technical and artificial sense completely at variance with their ordinary and natural meaning.
>
> (ibid., pp. 104–5)

Ryan qualified his recommendation by asking for an assurance that there was an identifiable code of generally accepted accounting principles. Failing this assurance he submitted as a personal recommendation that a statutory body be constituted under the Companies Act to make regulations as to the form and content of accounts and as to the accounting principles to be applied in their preparation. The body would be constituted of representatives of the legal, accountancy and secretarial professions and representatives of government. Ryan was thus not disagreeing with the ICAA that truth and fairness could be attained via GAAP but doubted both that such a body of principles *currently* existed and that the accountancy profession would be able to develop one.

The general tone of the debate was thus unfriendly to the true and fair concept and the participants notably failed to provide a complete list of 'excuses' for departing from the existing inadequate requirements. In particular there was no proposal that legislation might be amended explicitly to allow companies to depart from the detailed requirements of the Act in the interest of truth and fairness. Such an amendment could strengthen a profession which controls accounting standards and which can through the audit function define permissible departures from true and fair in terms of accounting standards. This is the model towards which the UK accountancy profession was moving, but it was doing so at a time when Australian eyes were turning away from the UK towards America. Moreover, as we shall see later, the Australian profession had little faith in its ability to demonstrate that it could persuade companies to comply with its recommendations and standards.

What clearly did emerge from the debate was that, despite the diversity of views, all the participants were agreed that Australian financial reporting needed a better set of rules. The role of the rules was, however, not agreed. They might serve (a) as a necessary and sufficient condition for truth and fairness, or (b) as a necessary but not sufficient condition for truth and fairness, or (c) as sufficient in themselves without any reference needed to truth and fairness. We turn next therefore to a brief account of Australian attempts to tidy up and extend the body of accounting rules. Here again we can observe a process of deharmonization with the UK as American models become increasingly influential.

EXTENDING THE RULES

Although they did not cooperate in their issue of statements on accounting principles and practice until 1972, in 1965 the Institute of Chartered Accountants in Australia and the Australian Society of Accountants joined forces to establish the Accountancy Research Foundation (later renamed the Australian Accounting Research Foundation (AARF)) (Zeff, 1973, pp. 43–9). Its first substantial research effort was W.J. Kenley's *A Statement of Australian Accounting Principles* (1970), an attempt to summarize and synthesize accounting principles which, significantly, was based not on any UK model but on the similar US study by Paul Grady. Kenley later went on to collaborate with the US academic George Staubus to produce *Objectives and Concepts of Financial Statements* (1972).

In the field of accounting regulation, the Commonwealth and State governments set up a Company Law Advisory Committee in 1967 under the chairmanship of Mr Justice Eggleston. The Eggleston Committee reported in 1970, and in line with its recommendations the Uniform Companies Act was amended in all States in 1971. The requirements as to the contents of the accounts and the directors' report were considerably increased and directors were required to comply with the detailed provisions of the Ninth Schedule. If compliance resulted in a true and fair view not being given, directors had to supply extra information to ensure that a true and fair view was given.

In regulatory circles in NSW there were few doubts about the need for extending and strengthening GAAP. In 1970 the companies Registry was replaced by a Corporate Affairs Commission with F.J.O. Ryan as the first Commissioner. In 1972 he envisaged the possibility of an approach to the NSW Supreme Court for a ruling as to what constituted generally accepted accounting principles. In 1974 the Commission began selective examination of company accounts for breaches of the Companies Act and compliance with Statements of Accounting Standards issued by the ICAA and ASA. From 1976 the Commission adopted the view that accounts not prepared according to the standards were prima facie not true and fair.

It became increasingly clear in the 1970s and early 1980s (e.g. from evidence published in the Reports of the NSW Commissioner: see Chambers, 1978, pp. 58–62; Walker, 1987, p. 270) that the ICAA's Recommendations were not being complied with. Action was taken both by the profession and by the NSW government, which set up an Accounting Standards Review Committee chaired by R.J. Chambers of the University of Sydney. The Committee's Report, *Company Accounting Standards* (1978), concluded that accounting standards should be given statutory endorsement but did not consider that those that presently existed should be so endorsed.

In 1972 the ICAA issued Statement K1, 'Conformity with Institute Technical Statements' (the ASA issuing its equivalent Statement 300). According to these statements, accounting standards were designed to 'introduce a definitive approach to the concept of what gives a true and fair view' although it was admitted by the ICAA in its Statement of Accounting Practice on 'Presentation of the Balance Sheet' that, 'There may be very rare circumstances in the preparation of the accounts in which adherence to an Accounting Standard does not in the auditor's view produce a true and fair view.'

The changing wording of K1 forms part of the history of true and fair in Australia. A 1976 revision required that all departures from standards be disclosed in the accounts or in the auditor's report. A 1978 revision limited disclosure of departures from standards to those that were 'material'. Further amendments followed in 1979 when the statement was re-issued as APS 1, retaining, however, the reference to true and fair. In 1985 APS 1 was reviewed to require departures from standards to be disclosed in the financial statements and auditors' report. In 1990 it was reissued in a form that made it clear that both accounting standards and the profession's Statements of Accounting Concepts (SACs) were mandatory requirements for members of the Institute and the Society, with standards prevailing over concepts statements in the event of incompatibility. The issue of the concepts statements enabled the AARF, as we shall see later, to argue that the existence of an explicit conceptual framework made the requirement to give a true and fair view unnecessary. Strong opposition from companies led, however, to the withdrawal of the mandatory status of SACs in late 1993.

From 1979 onwards the ICAA and the ASA sought to solve the compliance problem by seeking statutory endorsement of the profession's accounting standards, making a joint submission to this effect to the Campbell Inquiry into the Australian Financial System. The Campbell Report recommended instead the establishment of an Accounting Standards Review Board.

Throughout the 1970s there were demands for reform to companies and securities legislation. The Rae Committee Report in 1974 had recommended the establishment of a national regulatory body. In the Australian context this meant an argument about the role of the states and whether federal intervention was necessary. After much discussion a compromise cooperative scheme for the regulation of companies was reached involving *inter alia* the creation of a National Companies and Securities Commission (which commenced operations in 1980), the operating arms of which were to be the State Corporate Affairs Commissions. At the same time a more national approach to company law was achieved by means of a Companies Act applying in the Australian Capital Territory with almost identical Companies Codes for each State.

An Accounting Standards Review Board was set up to approve 'applicable approved accounting standards' and companies were required to prepare accounts in accordance with these standards which were thus given legislative backing. The strength of the standards was weakened by provisions in the amending Act of 1983 (see Appendix 5.1) which allowed directors not to comply with an applicable approved accounting standard if to do so in their opinion would result in the accounts not giving a true and fair view. The reasons for, and the quantified financial effect of any non-compliance had to be stated. These provisions were the first *explicitly* to allow a departure from a regulation in order to give a true and fair view but they differed from the provisions of the UK Companies Act 1981 in that they referred only to accounting standards and that they allowed departure rather than obligated it.

The cooperative scheme and the simultaneous existence of the ASRB's standards and those issued by the profession (AASs) caused many problems (Parker, Peirson and Ramsay, 1987; Walker, 1987) and in the late 1980s the cooperative scheme was replaced by a national scheme and co-regulation by the public and private sectors. The ASRB and the Accounting Standards Board of the AARF merged in 1988. After some dispute a Corporations Law was enacted in all the states to operate as if it were a federal law and a federal Australian Securities Commission was established. The Corporate Affairs Commissions were replaced with state regional offices and state business centres (Miller, 1991).

THE DEBATE ON TRUE AND FAIR REVIVES

The NCSC provoked debate on many accounting issues through the publication in 1983 of a Green Paper on the 'Financial Reporting Requirements of the Companies Act and Codes'. *Inter alia*, it indicated (p. 26) that it was:

considering whether a statutory definition of 'true and fair view' by reference to (i) the purposes of financial statements, and (ii) the persons primarily intended to be served by those statements – or a wholly new requirement – might give more precise guidance to directors and auditors in discharging their responsibilities under sections 269 and 285 of the Act.

The Green Paper appeared at a time when, as in the UK, the context of the true and fair concept was shifting away from a concern with the inadequacies of historical cost accounting and towards a concern with the outrages of creative accounting.

The debate on true and fair began again in Australia when the NCSC commissioned a consultative document from Professor R.G. Walker, an accounting academic from the University of New South Wales who was one of the original members of the ASRB and also well known for his financial journalism.

Unlike the debate of the 1960s and 1970s, this second debate was not one which might equally have appeared in British accounting journals. Not only was Australia increasingly looking towards the USA, the UK in its turn was being influenced in its attitude to true and fair by the harmonizing activities of the European Community. Faced with the inevitability of a Fourth Directive which would impose more detailed measurement and presentation requirements, the reaction of the British profession was to strengthen the true and fair requirement as a defence. In the words of one of the UK negotiators:

> One of the safeguards against the degree of detail we are going to have to live with, *is* to get these words [true and fair view] in, because they enable us to override that detail where it is necessary for fair presentation.
>
> (Grenside, 1974, p. 30)

Thus UK accountants substantially survived the implementation of the Directive by, *inter alia*, 'the use of the "true and fair view" by the accountancy profession as a way of avoiding or being more restrictive than the Act' (Nobes and Parker, 1984, p. 94). True and fair came in the 1970s

> to represent the embodiment of the British view of accounting. If British concerns were to prevail, the discretionary powers of the auditor and the accounting profession must also prevail, rather than regulation by the State ... the phraseology of true and fair had to be imbued with the full significance of the underlying dispute over the territorial claims as to who should regulate and

influence accounting and how that influence should be exercised.

(Hopwood, 1990, p. 85)

As pointed out by Kenley (1984, p. 98), an Australian accountant writing in a British journal, the legislative requirements as to truth and fairness ceased to be the same in the UK and Australia. By taking part in the process of harmonization within the EC, the UK deharmonized with Australia.

The UK legislation was amended in 1981 to state explicitly that the requirement to give a true and fair view 'overrides' the [detailed] requirements of Schedule 4 and 'all other requirements of this Act as to the matters to be included in a company's accounts or notes to those accounts'. Accordingly, the Act continues, 'additional information must be provided' (not 'may' be provided) if the balance sheet or profit and loss account drawn up with the said requirements would not provide sufficient information to give a true and fair view. Furthermore, if 'owing to special circumstances' (undefined), compliance with the detailed requirements would result in not giving a true and fair view (even if additional information were provided) the directors must (not may) depart from that requirement. Particulars of any departure and the reasons therefore must be given in the notes.[1] The British legislation thus, unlike the Australian legislation, explicitly envisages departures from the detailed accounting requirements of the Companies Act, not just from applicable accounting standards.

Renshall (1982) explains clearly why the 1981 amendments were more than just a reaffirmation of the primacy of the true and fair view enshrined in the 1948 Act and copied by the Australian States:

> The old Sch 8 was intentionally no more than a minimum list of items to be disclosed in accounts. Mere adherence to old Sch 8 could not of itself ensure that a true and fair view was given. The new Sch 8 not only sets out a minimum list of information to be provided: it spells out the precise way in which the information is to be presented, and the basic measurement rules.
>
> (Renshall, 1982, p. 20)

As already noted, the equivalent of Schedule 8 in Australian legislation has remained a list of disclosure rules, although formats have been introduced.

In writing his consultative document Walker was able to draw on not only the Australian debate of the 1960s and 1970s and on his knowledge of developments in the UK, but also on two papers published in Australia in the early 1980s. J.B. Ryan (1980), writing in a *Festschrift* in honour of Johnston, argued for the retention of a true and fair view as the overriding requirement in order to preserve 'the need for the exercise of professional judgment in the application of standards by directors, guided by their accountants, in the first instance, and by auditors, in the second'. He recommended the inclusion in the Companies Act of a section stating that, subject to the overriding requirement for accounts to give a true and fair view, non-compliance with accounting standards will constitute prima facie evidence that the accounts may not show a true and fair view, or more positively, that compliance with accounting standards will constitute prima facie evidence that the accounts do give a true and fair view.

Forster (1983, p. 11) warned of the dangers of trying to define a true and fair view: 'Setting out to *define* what true and fair *means* in the context of the Companies Code would be simply to construct a legal latticework through which the unscrupulous would then proceed to drive the proverbial horse and cart.' He argued that true and fair should be treated as a single concept, i.e. as a 'hendiadys', and interpreted literally not technically.

Walker was also aware that, in March 1984, before the publication of his consultative document, the accountancy bodies' Auditing Standards Board (AuSB) had published a revised Statement of Auditing Practice 3 (AUP3) which recommended the amendment of the Companies Act so as to make possible a standard form audit report on the following lines: 'In our opinion, the financial statements present fairly the financial position of . . . at . . . and the results of its operations for the year then ended in accordance with Australian Accounting Standards (and comply with . . .)'. This audit report appears to be modelled on the US report with 'in accordance with Australian Accounting Standards' substituted for 'in conformity with generally accepted accounting principles'. Pending amendment of the Act, it was recommended that the audit report of a company should state in part that:

In our opinion:

1 the accounts are properly drawn up in accordance with the provisions of (Companies Act 1981/relevant State Companies Code) and so as to give a true and fair view of:
   (i) the state of affairs of the company at . . . and of the profit (or loss) of the company for the year ended on that date;
   (ii) the other matters required by Section 269 of that Act/Code to be dealt with in the accounts;
   and are in accordance with Australian Accounting Standards and applicable approved accounting standards.

AUP3 was no doubt issued partly as a lobbying device (Psaros and Oliver, 1986, p. 41).

According to the AuSB's Explanatory Memorandum it was difficult to achieve 'any definitive meaning or consensus in the use and communicative effectiveness of "true and fair". To continue to pursue a reporting form which uses words which have a technical and artificial context, which is at variance with their ordinary and natural meaning, would in the view of the board, be ineffective.'

The AuSB's standards were clearly influenced by US rather than UK precedents as Australian auditors from 1968 onwards turned towards America (Gibson and Arnold, 1981) but, as Walker (1984, pp. 50–3) pointed out, AUP3 did not address the problem of whether 'present fairly' (or 'true and fair') 'in accordance with' means *and* in accordance with, *because* they are in accordance with, *to the extent that* they are in accordance with, or *presented* in accordance with accounting standards, consistently applied. Walker's recommendation to the NCSC was the insertion of a clause in the Companies Act defining a true and fair view as follows:

> Without affecting the generality of the meaning of the term '*true and fair view*', a 'true and fair view' in relation to accounts or group accounts means a representation which affords those who might reasonably be expected to refer to those accounts (including holders or prospective purchasers of shares, debentures, notes or other interests, and creditors or prospective creditors) information which is relevant to the decisions which may be made by those persons in relation to the purchase, sale or other action in connection with their securities or interests.
>
> (Walker, 1984, p. 28)

In making this recommendation Walker sought, he said, to retain the substance of the true and fair requirement but to amplify it, by eliminating ambiguity, in the hope that the requirement would become more readily enforceable.

Walker's recommendation was supported by Wolnizer (1985), an academic accountant, but found no favour with the leaders of the accountancy profession. In a submission to the NCSC (see Pound, 1985a, b; Edwards, 1985) prepared by the Auditing Standards Board of the AARF, the accountancy bodies argued that the recommendation would not:

1 clarify the meaning of true and fair view in relation to financial reporting;

2 properly or effectively identify the groups intended to be served by financial reporting;
3 make more enforceable any action arising from non-compliance with the requirement to give a true and fair view;

and that, further, the suggested amendment proposed 'that accounts should contain information which is relevant to an undefined but seemingly all inclusive group of users for an undefined (but seemingly all inclusive) range of purposes'. Walker's amendment was, in the opinion of the Australian Society's president (Edwards, 1985) 'inappropriate and impractical and would place an impossible responsibility on accountants, auditors and directors'. The AARF had therefore recommended to the NCSC a modified version of AUP3, viz. that the auditors should report that accounts 'present fairly . . . in accordance with approved accounting standards and comply with the Companies Code' with a similar wording for the Statement by Directors. Accounting standards, AARF claimed, provided an identifiable framework within which an audit opinion could be framed. This would not merely be the 'application of a set of rules' because accounting standards contained qualitative criteria.

Walker's recommendation was also attacked by J.B. Ryan as 'misconceived' . . . and likely to increase uncertainty and confusion' (Ryan, 1985, p. 11). Replying vigorously to Ryan and to his critics in the profession, Walker (1986, p. 34) argued that detailed rules could not be expected to cover every circumstance or every situation. An overriding requirement was needed to fill any gaps in detailed reporting requirements. Much of the detail in Schedule 7 had been introduced to amplify the general true and fair reporting requirements not to replace them. Compliance with a set of detailed rules would not guarantee that the information contained in accounting statements was not misleading. The argument for the abandonment of the true and fair requirement was an argument for change 'in the interests of auditors and preparers of financial statements, at the expense of those who stand to benefit from the dissemination of high quality information'.

Despite Walker's arguments, amendments were made to the Corporations Law in June 1991 which require compliance first with applicable Australian Accounting Standards Board (AASB) standards and then the addition of whatever information and explanations are necessary to give a true and fair view. Directors are no longer permitted to depart from standards where they consider compliance would result in financial statements which do not give a true and fair view.

The result of these changes in the law as characterized by the executive director of the AARF as follows:

the financial statements as a whole must now both give a true and fair view and comply with accounting standards (and Schedule 5) rather than *merely* give a true and fair view and comply with only those accounting standards which the directors believe are consistent with giving a true and fair view.

(McGregor, 1992, p. 69).

McGregor argued strongly that the true and fair concept has often been *misused* (by being used to justify non-compliance with accounting rules) or *ignored* (by being applied as meaning conformity with minimum legal requirements). He saw no hope of preventing this and proposed instead that the true and fair requirement be replaced with a requirement to: 'present fairly the financial position of operations of the company in accordance with Statements of Accounting Concepts and Accounting Standards' (ibid., p. 71). This proposal, claimed McGregor, is broadly consistent with the approaches followed in the United States and Canada where 'Non-compliance is not tolerated by the securities regulators and enforcement problems as we know them in Australia are non-existent' (ibid.). True and fair was thus in McGregor's eyes an accounting anachronism whose role had been replaced by that of an explicit conceptual framework as set out in the Statements of Accounting Concepts, which, it will be recalled, had at the date he was writing mandatory status for members of the Institute and Society. In late 1993, however, as a result of strongly voiced objections from Australian companies, this mandatory status was withdrawn.

This line of thought is discussed by Hines (1987) who quotes US evidence of the difficulty of using conceptual frameworks to resolve accounting issues and casts doubt on whether accounting standards and rules can be legitimated in this way. Her preferred approach is to strengthen the standard-setting body by strengthening the 'due process' procedures, i.e. the steps used to ensure that an administrative decision is given the careful consideration that it should receive in order adequately to protect the interests of those affected by its decisions.

It may be doubted, however, whether either McGregor's or Hines' proposals would deal with the problem of 'creative compliance', i.e. using the law to escape legal control without actually violating legal rules (McBarnet and Whelan, 1991). As Bosch (1990, p. 31) pointed out, reviewing his period as chairman of the NCSC:

One of the great problems with detailed codes of black-letter law is that they provide scope for clever lawyers to find loopholes. There have been many cases of outrageous behaviour that cannot be attacked because the schemes have been carefully constructed to stay just within the letter of the law.

DID TRUE AND FAIR 'FAIL'?

According to Miller (1991, p. 36) the true and fair view criterion failed 'to discipline the reporting process, as was demonstrated by the outrages perpetrated in the eighties' and he refers his readers to descriptions of some of these outrages by Sykes (1990), a financial journalist, and by Bosch (1990, ch. 12). But would the outrages have been less if the 1991 amendments to the Corporations Act had been in place in the 1980s?

As Tweedie (1988) points out, the true and fair concept is potentially both progressive and regressive. In its progressive form it can be used to replace antiquated laws and standards. This is the way the technical partners of the large UK auditing firms claim to see it (Parker and Nobes, 1991). In its regressive form, however, the concept may hold back progressive auditors who:

> cannot simply qualify their reports if they believe a practice used by a client and in general use by other companies in the same industry is perhaps no longer suitable. They are constrained by the acceptance of prevailing practice by their colleagues. The corollary is that if what may be deemed to be a poor accounting treatment evolves and is accepted by two or three of the major firms it becomes increasingly difficult, both conceptually and commercially, for the next accounting firm to take a different line and qualify its report. Indeed its clients may feel that they are at an economic disadvantage were the firm to do so and in such cases they could certainly demand to know why their auditor was taking a view contrary to others in the profession. As a result, what could be deemed poor practice or creative accounting can become accepted, however reluctantly, by many of the major firms who may feel at a commercial disadvantage if they take a stand against a practice which they dislike but which is accepted by many of their competitors (and hence, it is argued, becomes part of the practices encompassed by the true and fair view) and much approved of by their clients.
>
> (Tweedie, 1988, pp. 2–3)

This is a long way from Bosch's (1990, p. 33) apocryphal story of an old auditor who carried out his audits by taking his family bible into board meetings and having each director in turn swear to the truth and fairness of the company's accounts.

Tweedie's analysis suggests that whether the progressive or regressive aspect of the true and fair concept prevails depends on the morality of the preparers and auditors of financial statements. Comparisons of morality are difficult to make but Australian standard-setters have certainly shown themselves less willing than those in the UK to accept that the progressive form of the concept can operate in practice. McGregor (1992) refers to widespread non-compliance with approved accounting standards accompanied by a virtually complete disregard by companies and auditors of the requirement to explain why compliance would not give a true and fair view. He goes on to refer to the extreme reluctance by regulators to prosecute because of the difficulties of defining a true and fair view.

Why have UK and Australian standard-setters taken such different attitudes to the true and fair view requirement? The simplest explanation, couched in the language of territorial claims, is that to UK professional standard-setters true and fair has represented an opportunity whereas to Australian professional standard-setters it has been seen as a threat. The crucial difference is that, as a result of the amendments brought about via the Fourth Directive, truth and fairness could be used in the UK to depart from the detailed requirements of company legislation whereas in Australia it could only be used to depart from applicable accounting standards. The UK Accounting Standards Committee used the true and fair override to ban LIFO in SSAP 9 although it is specifically allowed by the Companies Act; to require in SSAP 19 investment properties not to be depreciated whereas the Act requires all fixed assets with limited useful lives to be depreciated; and in SSAP20 to require the taking of gains on unsettled long-term foreign currency loans to profit and loss account although this is not 'prudent' and prudence is a mandatory principle in the Act. Furthermore, UK auditing firms appear to interpret the true and fair override as meaning the primacy of accounting standards and, in the absence of accounting standards, a professional consensus (e.g. on marking to market) (Parker and Nobes, 1991). UK auditors and standard-setters thus appear to see the true and fair override as a way of overriding the detailed requirements of the Act but not as a way of overriding accounting standards. The ASB has stated that it 'envisages that only in exceptional circumstances will departure from the requirements of an accounting standard be necessary in order for financial statements to give a true and fair view' (Foreword to *Accounting Standards*, June 1993, para. 18) and has obtained counsel's opinion to the effect that the reconstitution of the membership of the standard-setting body so that it no longer simply reflects the views of the accountancy profession, its partial funding by the government, and its statutory recognition, have increased the likelihood that the Courts will hold that, in general, compliance with accounting standards is necessary to meet the true and fair requirement. (*Accountancy*, July 1993, pp. 122–3.)

This contrasts strongly with the experience of Australian professional standard-setters who are unable to use their standards to override the detailed requirements of the Act (although these, it will be recalled, include very few measurement rules) and have seen their standards departed from to a much greater extent than in the UK by companies and auditors on the grounds of truth and fairness (the evidence for non-compliance with accounting standards is set out in the articles cited in Deegan *et al.*, 1990, p. 264, n. 8). Even the amendments to the law in 1991 have not prevented this. Some Australian companies have presented two sets of financial statements: one set in accordance with accounting standards, the other set 'true and fair' (*Charter*, April 1993, pp. 4–5).

Also, in the UK the accountancy profession has not been faced with an attempt to define true and fair view in a way perceived to increase auditors' liability. It is not surprising that the Australian profession should be opposed to a recommendation that has an 'effect on the potential civil liability of those who prepare and audit financial statements' (Walker, 1992).

Those who wish to change regulations need 'excuses'. UK accountants in the 1970s operated in an environment in which the true and fair concept was widely accepted and subjected to little critical discussion. In the UK, the *lack* of a debate of the kind which took place in Australia in the 1960s and 1970s made the regulatory changes easier to introduce, especially as they could be portrayed as the triumph of the UK flexible approach against continental European rigidity. By contrast, the present Australian opponents of the true and fair requirement are able to look back on debates, carried on mainly by academics and regulators, which, as already noted, have generally been unfriendly to the concept, and to pick the 'excuse' which coincides most nearly with the policy that they wish to adopt. McGregor (1992) states that his preferred solution is that of Baxt (1968) who argued, as we have seen, that accounting principles should be spelled out in the law, but his solution is perhaps closer to that supported by Ryan (1967) and Heazlewood (1971). If it were to be adopted, and accepted by Australian companies, deharmonization with UK accounting in this area would be complete and the Australian debate on true and fair would be settled. That the debate continues is shown by the publication in 1993 of an AARF discussion paper on qualitative standards for financial reporting (Sadhu and Langfield-Smith, 1993).

AN EXERCISE IN DEHARMONIZATION?

There is no doubt that Australian and UK financial reporting have been deharmonized so far as the true and fair concept is concerned. Accounting standard-setters in the two countries have gone separate ways in response to different environments. These differences include the UK's entry into the European Community and Australia's increasing movement, both economically and culturally, towards the USA and away from the UK. Standard-setters in the UK have had an incentive as part of the harmonization process to support a strengthening and extension of the true and fair requirement. Australian standard-setters, on the other hand, have been strongly influenced by pressures towards harmonization with the USA and deharmonization with the UK, but in the process have attempted to evolve a unique Australian solution by attempting (as neither UK nor US standard-setters have) to put conceptual statements on the same footing as statements of accounting standards. That solution did not, however, survive strong opposition from Australian companies who have preferred harmonization in this respect with the US and the UK. There appears to be a limit to Australian companies' willingness to deharmonize with both UK and US accounting. As the group chief accountant of a leading Australian company has put it: 'Australia must not allow its accounting concepts to get in front of the "world pack"' (Philp, 1993, p. 20).

APPENDIX 5.1

Extracts from Australian Companies Acts

Uniform Companies Acts 1961–1962

162(11)   Every balance-sheet . . . shall give a true and fair view of the state of affairs of the company as at the end of the period to which it relates and every profit and loss account . . . shall give a true and fair view of the profit or loss of the company for the period of accounting as shown in the accounting and other records of the company, and without affecting the generality of the foregoing, every such balance-sheet and profit and loss account shall comply with the requirements of the Ninth Schedule so far as applicable thereto . . .

162(12)   Every balance-sheet and profit and loss account of a company shall be accompanied by a statement signed on behalf of the directors by two directors of the company, or in the case of a proprietary company having one director only, by that director, stating that in their or his opinion –

(a)   the profit and loss account is drawn up so as to give a true and fair view of the results of the business of the company for the period covered by the account; and

(b)   the balance-sheet is drawn up so as to exhibit a true and fair view of the state of affairs of the company as at the end of that period.

167(1)   Every auditor of a company shall report to the members as to every balance-sheet and profit and loss account laid before the company in general meeting during his tenure of office and shall state in the report whether, in his opinion –

(a)   the balance-sheet and profit and loss account are properly drawn up in accordance with the provisions of this Act and so as to give a true and fair view of the state of the company's affairs;

. . .

1971 Companies Acts

162(9)   Without affecting the generality of the preceding provisions of this section, the accounts of a company and, if it is a holding company for which group accounts are required, the group accounts shall comply with such of the requirements of the Ninth Schedule as are applicable to them, but where accounts or group accounts prepared in accordance with these requirements would not otherwise give a true and fair view of the matters required by this section to be dealt with in the accounts or group accounts, the directors of the company shall add such information and explanations as will give a true and fair view of those matters.

1981 Companies Act and Codes

269(1)   The directors of a company shall . . . cause to be made out a profit and loss account . . . that gives a true and fair view of the profit or loss of the company for that financial year.

(2)   The directors of a company shall . . . cause to be made out a balance-sheet . . . that gives a true and fair view of the state of affairs of the company as at the end of that financial year.

. . .

(8)   Without affecting the generality of the preceding provisions of this section, the directors of a company shall ensure that the accounts of the company, and if it is a holding company for which group accounts are required, the group accounts comply with such of the prescribed requirements as are relevant to these accounts or group accounts, as the case may be, but where accounts or group accounts prepared in accordance with these requirements would not otherwise give a true and fair view of the matters required by this section to be dealt with in the accounts or group accounts, the directors of the company shall add such information and explanations as will give a true and fair view of those matters.

(8A)   Without affecting the generality of the preceding provisions of this section, the directors of a company shall ensure that the accounts of the company and if the company is a holding company for which group accounts are required, the group accounts of the company are made out in accordance with applicable approved accounting standards. [inserted 1983]

(8B) Notwithstanding sub-section (8A), where the accounts of a company or the group accounts of a holding company would not, if made out in accordance with a particular approved accounting standard, give a true and fair view of the matters required by this section to be dealt with in those accounts or group accounts, as the case may be, the directors of the company or holding company are not required to ensure that those accounts or group accounts, as the case may be, are made out in accordance with that accounting standard. [inserted 1983]

(9) The directors of a company shall . . .

    (a) [state] whether, in the opinion of the directors –

        (i) the profit and loss account is drawn up so as to give a true and fair view of the profit or loss of the company for its last financial year . . .

        (ii) the balance-sheet is drawn up so as to give a true and fair view of the state of affairs of the company as at the end of the financial year . . .

    (b) [state] whether the accounts have been made out in accordance with applicable approved accounting standards;

    (c) if the accounts have not been made out in accordance with a particular applicable approved accounting standard –

        (i) [state]why the accounts, if made out in accordance with that accounting standard, would not have given a true and fair view . . ., and

        (ii) [give] particulars of the quantified financial effect on the accounts of the failure to make out the accounts in accordance with that accounting standard . . . [inserted 1983]

(10) [similarly for group accounts] [inserted 1983]

Corporations Law, 1989 (amended 1991)

292 A company's directors shall before the deadline after a financial year cause to be made out a profit and loss account for that financial year that gives a true and fair view of the company's profit for that financial year.

293 A company's directors shall, before the deadline after a financial year, cause to be made out a balance-sheet as at the end of that financial year that gives a true and fair view of the company's state of affairs as at the end of that financial year.

297(1) A company's directors shall ensure that the company's financial statements for a financial year comply with such of the prescribed requirements as are relevant to the financial statements.

297(2) When a company's financial statements for a financial year, as prepared in accordance with subsection (1), would not otherwise give a true and fair view of the matters with which this Division requires them to deal, the directors shall add such information and explanations as will give a true and fair view of those matters. [deleted 1.8.91]

298(1)   Subject to section 297, a company's directors shall ensure that the company's financial statements for a financial year are made out in accordance with applicable accounting standards.

298(2)   Despite subsection (1), where a company's financial statements for a financial year would not, if made out in accordance with a particular applicable accounting standard, give a true and fair view of the matters with which this Division requires the financial statements to deal, the directors need not ensure that the financial statements are made out in accordance with that accounting standard. [deleted 1.8.91]

299(1)   If a company's financial statements for a financial year, as prepared in accordance with sections 297 and 298, would not otherwise give a true and fair view of the matters with which this Part requires them to deal, the directors must add such information and explanation as will give a true and fair view of these matters. [inserted 1.8.91]

NOTES

1   For extracts from relevant British Companies Acts to 1985 see Nobes and Parker (1991a), App. A. The 1985 Act was amended in 1989 to make it clear that a departure was independent of the giving of additional information.

REFERENCES

Alexander, F. (1972), *Australia Since Federation*, Melbourne: Nelson, rev. edn.

Baxt, R. (1968), 'True and fair view: a legal analysis', *Accountant's Journal* (NZ), April, pp. 301–10.

Baxt, R. (1970), 'True and fair accounts: a legal anachronism', *Australian Law Journal*, 30 November.

Birkett, W.P. (1968), 'True and fair – the law and accounting', *Australian Lawyer*, 15 May.

Bosch, H. (1990), *The Workings of a Watchdog*, Melbourne: Heinemann Australia.

Buchanan, W. and Cantril, H. (1953), *How Nations See Each Other*, Urbana: University of Illinois; reprinted Westport, Conn.: Greenwood Press, 1972).

Chambers, R.J. (Chairman) (1978), *Company Accounting Standards. Report of the Accounting Standards Review Committee*, Ultimo, NSW: Government Printer.

Chastney, J.G. (1975), *True and Fair View – History, Meaning and the Impact of the Fourth Directive*, London: Institute of Chartered Accountants in England and Wales.

Deegan, C., Morris, R. and Stokes, D. (1990), 'Audit firm lobbying on proposed disclosure requirements', *Australian Journal of Management*, December.

Dyer, J.C. IV (1974), 'The meaning of true in "true and fair"', *Australian Business Law Review*, September, pp. 187–203.

Edey, H.C. (1971), 'The true and fair view', *Accountancy*, August.

Edwards, B. (1985), '"True and fair" – not just an academic debate', *Australian Accountant*, March.

Forster, A.A. (1983), 'The will-o'-the wisp of true and fair', *Professional Administrator*, Jan–March.

Gibson, R.W. (1971), *Disclosure by Australian Companies*, Melbourne: Melbourne University Press.

Gibson, R.W., and Arnold, R. (1981), The development of auditing standards in Australia', *Accounting Historians Journal*, Spring, reprinted in Parker (1990).

Grenside, J. (interviewed Lafferty, M.) (1974), 'Fourth Directive ... what's in it for us?', *Accountancy*, July.

Heazlewood, C.T. (1971), 'True and fair and the Companies (Amendment) Bill 1970', *Chartered Accountant in Australia*, April.

Hines, R. (1987), 'Financial accounting standard setting: from truth to due process', *Chartered Accountant in Australia*, July, pp. 3–33.

Hopwood, A.G. (1990), 'Ambiguity, knowledge and territorial claims: some observations on the doctrine of substance over form: a review essay', *British Accounting Review*, March.

Horrocks, J. (1967), 'Are published balance sheets untrue and unfair?', *Australian Accountant*, October.

Houghton, K.A. (1987), 'True and fair view: an empirical study of connotative meaning', *Accounting, Organizations and Society*, vol. 12, no. 2.

Irish, R.A. (1966), 'Trial by fire', *Chartered Accountant in Australia*, September.

Johnston, T.R. (1967), 'Is the standard "true and fair view of the state of affairs" attainable in a balance sheet?', *Accountant's Journal* (NZ), July, pp. 443–52.

Johnston, T.R., and Jager, M.O. (1963), *The Law and Practice of Company Accounting in Australia* (Sydney: Butterworths).

Kenley, J. (1984), 'True and fair rules – some Australian observations', *Accountant's Magazine*, March.

Kenley, W.J. (1970), *A Statement of Australian Accounting Principles*, Australian Accounting Research Foundation.

Kenley, W.J. and Staubus, G. (1972), *Objectives and Concepts of Financial Statements*, Australian Accounting Research Foundation.

Kettle, R. (1950), 'Balance sheets and accounts under the Companies Act, 1948', in Baxter, W.T. (ed.), *Studies in Accounting*, London: Sweet and Maxwell.

McBarnet, D. and Whelan, C. (1991), 'The elusive spirit of the law: formalism and the struggle for legal control', *Modern Law Review*, November.

McGregor, W. (1992), 'True and fair – an accounting anachronism', *Australian Accountant*, February, *AAARF Report*, March.

Miller, M.C. (1969), '"True and fair" and auditors' reports', *Australian Accountant*, April.

Miller, M. (1991), 'Shifts in the regulatory framework for corporate financial reporting', *Australian Accounting Review*, November.

Moore, W.H. (1934), 'A century of Victorian law', *Journal of Comparative Legislation and International Law*, 3rd ser., vol. 16.

Nobes, C.W. (1993), 'The true and fair view: impact on and of the Fourth Directive', *Accounting and Business Research*, Winter.

Nobes, C.W. and Parker, R.H. (1984), 'The Fourth Directive and the United Kingdom', in Gray, S.J. and Coenenberg, A.G., *EEC Accounting Harmonisation: Implementation and Impact of the Fourth Directive*, Amsterdam: North Holland.

Nobes, C.W. and Parker, R.G. (1991a), '"True and fair": a survey of UK financial directors', *Journal of Business Finance and Accounting*, April.

Nobes, C.W. and Parker, R.H. (1991b), *Comparative International Accounting*, Hemel Hempstead: Prentice Hall, 3rd edn.

Parker, R.H. (1989), 'Importing and exporting accounting: the British experience' in Hopwood, A.G. (ed.), *International Pressures for Accounting Change*, London: Prentice-Hall.

Parker, R.H. (ed.) (1990), *Accounting in Australia. Historical Essays*, New York: Garland.

Parker, R.H. and Nobes, C.W. (1991), 'Auditors' view of true and fair', *Accounting and Business Research*, Autumn.

Parker, R.H., Peirson, G. and Ramsay, A.L. (1987), 'Australian accounting standards and the law', *Companies and Securities Law Journal*, November.

Peasnell, K.V. and Williams, D.J. (1986), 'Ersatz academics and scholar-saints: the supply of financial accounting research', *Abacus*, September.

Philp, R. (1993), 'Comment: out of step', *Australian Accounting Review*, May.

Pound, G.D. (1985a), 'Reporting obligations of auditors', *Australian Accountant*, March.

Pound, G.D. (1985b), 'True and fair debate – accounting bodies reply', *Chartered Accountant in Australia*, March.

Psaros, J. and Oliver, B. (1986), 'Audit reports – does AUP3 provide adequate guidance?', *Chartered Accountant in Australia*, March.

Renshall, M. (1982), 'The Companies Act 1981 (1) changed aspects of accounting and disclosure: an accountant's view', *Company Lawyer*, January.

Ryan, F.J.O. (1974), 'A true and fair view revisited', *Australian Accountant*, February.

Ryan, F.J.O. (1967), 'A true and fair view', *Abacus*, December.

Ryan, J. (1985), 'A recipe for added confusion', *Australian Accountant*, September.

Ryan, J.B. (1980), 'A true and fair view: an accounting interpretation', in Emanuel, D. and Stewart, J., *Essays in Honour of Trevor R. Johnston*, University of Auckland Press.

Sadhu, M.A. and Langfield-Smith, I.A. (1993), *A Qualitative Standard for General Purpose Financial Reports: A Review*, Caulfield, Vic.: Australian Accounting Research Foundation, Legislative Discussion Paper.

Stamp, E. (1964), 'The Reid Murray Affair', *Accountant's Journal*, (NZ), May, *Accountancy*, August.

Sykes, T. (1990), 'True, fair or false?', *Australian Business*, 4 July.

Tweedie, D. (1988), 'True and fair v. the rule book: which is the answer to creative accounting?', *Pacific Accounting Review*, December.

Walker, R.G. (1984), '*A true and fair view' and the Reporting Obligations of Directors and Auditors*, Melbourne: National Companies and Securities Commission.

Walker, R.G. (1986), 'True and fair view revisited', *Australian Accountant*, April.

Walker, R.G. (1987), 'Australia's ASRB: a case study of political activity and regulatory "capture"', *Accounting and Business Research*, Summer.

Walker, R.G. (1992), 'Let's redefine – not dump – true and fair view', *New Accountant*, 15 October.

Watts, R.L. and Zimmerman, J.L. (1979), 'The demand for and supply of accounting theories: the market for excuses', *Accounting Review*, April.

Whittington, G. (1983), 'The role of research in setting accounting standards: the case of inflation accounting', in Bromwich, M. and Hopwood, A.G., *Accounting Standards Setting. An International Perspective*, London: Pitman.

Wolnizer, P. (1985), '"Correspondence with the facts" – a recurrent theme in commentaries on the statutory quality standard of truth and fairness in accounts', *Company and Securities Law Journal*, August.

Zeff, S.A. (1973), *Forging Accounting Principles in Australia*, Melbourne: Australian Society of Accountants Bulletin No. 14, reprinted in Parker (1990).

This paper by R.H. Parker was first published in the Journal of International Accounting, Auditing and Taxation, *July 1994.*

Bibliography of writings in English on true and fair, 1944–1993

We attempt below a comprehensive listing of books and articles in English (excluding those in newspapers) dealing with true and fair and written between 1944 (when the phrase was first suggested as a legal requirement) and 1993, inclusive. Writings on the US concept of 'fair presentation' are *not* included.

Accountant (1944), 'The Institute on Company Law – III', 1 July.

Accountant (1962), 'Candidates for truth', 27 January.

Accountant (1971), 'True and fair view? New look at traditional principles', 27 May.

Accountant (1973), 'True and fair in Europe', 12 April.

Accountant (1975), 'How fair is "true and fair?"', 8 May.

Accountants' Journal (NZ) (1982), 'Legal opinion on historic cost phrase', September.

Alexander, D. (1993), 'A European true and fair view?', *European Accounting Review*, May.

Anderson, J.V.R. (1976), '"True and Fair" in the EEC', *Accountant*, 4 March.

Arden, M. (1993), 'The true and fair requirement', in Accounting Standards Board, 'Preface to Accounting Standards', reprinted in *Accountancy*, July.

Ardwinckle, R. (1987), 'Off-balance sheet finance – the legal view', *Accountancy*, June.

Ashton, R.K. (1986), 'The Argyll Foods case. A legal analysis', *Accounting and Business Research*, Winter.

Balfour, D. (1984) (pseudonym), 'What price window dressing?', *Accountant's Magazine*, August.

Baxt, R. (1968), 'True and fair view – a legal analysis', *Accountants' Journal* (NZ), April.

Baxt, R. (1970), 'True and fair accounts: a legal anachronism', *Australian Law Journal*, vol. 44, 30 November.

Benson, H. (1962), 'Auditing and the world economy', *Accountancy*, November and December.

Bhattacharya, K. (1988), 'More or less true, quite fair', *Accountancy*, December.

Bird, P.A. (1982a), 'After Argyll Foods what is "a true and fair view"?', *Accountancy*, June.

Bird, P.A. (1982b), 'Group accounts and the true and fair view', *Journal of Business Law*, September.

Bird, P. (1984), 'What is "A true and fair view"?', *Journal of Business Law*, November.

Birkett, W.P. (1968), 'True and fair – the law and accounting', *Australian Lawyer*, May 1968.

Brady, N. and Healy, A. (1991), 'True and fair view increases debate over insurance accounting', *Accountant*, August.

Burlaud, A. (1993), 'Commentary on the article by David Alexander "A European true and fair view"', *European Accounting Review*, May.

Busse von Colbe, W. (1980), 'True and fair – the German way', *Accountancy Age*, 7 November.

Busse von Colbe, W. (1984), 'A true and fair view: a German perspective', in S.J. Gray and A.G. Coenenberg, *EEC Accounting Harmonisation*, North Holland.

Caie, R. (1971), 'Qualifications in audit reports: what is a "true and fair view"?', *Accountant*, 23 September.

Carnegie, G.D. and Gavens, J.J. (1989), 'NCSC Specific Relief Orders and a "true and fair view"', *Company and Securities Law Journal*, April.

Carslaw, C. (1984), 'It's not what you say, but the way that you say it', *Accountancy*, February.

Certified Accountant (1983), 'True and fair concept debate', October.

Certified Accountant (1983), 'But what exactly is true and fair?', November.

Chambers, R.J. and Wolnizer, P.W. (1990), 'A true and fair view of financial position', *Company and Securities Law Journal*, December.

Chambers, R.J. and Wolnizer, P.W. (1991), 'True and fair view of position and results: the historical background', *Acccounting, Business and Financial History*, March.

Chartered Accountant in Australia (1973), 'Multinationals – a true and fair view', September.

Chastney, J.G. (1975), *True and Fair View – History, Meaning and the Impact of the Fourth Directive*, Institute of Chartered Accountants in England and Wales.

Chopping, D. and Skerratt, L. (1993), 'True and fair', *Applying GAAP 1993/94*, Accountancy Books, ch. 3.

Clarke, F.L. (1984), 'Consumer protection: standards, and true and fair', *Accountant's Magazine*, November.

Cowan, T.K. (1965), 'Are truth and fairness generally acceptable?', *Accounting Review*, October.

Davison, I.H. (1983), *Accounting Standards, the True and Fair View and the Law*, Arthur Andersen & Co.

Demirag, I. and Macve, R. (1986a), 'A "true and fair view" and the treatment of long-term contract work in progress', *Accountant's Magazine*, June.

Demirag, I. and Macve, R. (1986b), 'Long-term contract work in progress: Can we resolve the conflict?', *Accountant's Magazine*, July.

Department of Trade (1982), 'The true and fair view and group accounts', *Accountant's Magazine*, February; *Accountancy*, February.

Dixon, S. (1969), 'A true and fair view', *Accountancy*, February.

Donleavy, G.D. (1990), 'Note on a test of students' grasp of truth and fairness before and after encountering funds statements', *British Accounting Review*, June.

Drayton, H. (1962), 'When is "fair" not fair? The auditor's report criticized', *Accountant*, 27 January.

Dyer, J.C. (1974), 'The meaning of true in "true and fair"', *Australian Business Law Review*, September.

Edey, H. (1971), 'The true and fair view', *Accountancy*, August.

Edwards, B. (1985), '"True and fair" – not just an academic debate', *Australian Accountant*, March.

Eggers, H.C. (1963), 'True and fair', *South African Accountant*, June.

Flint, D. (1978), 'A true and fair view in corporate reporting. Its meaning and significance', *Journal of the Law Society of Scotland*, December.

Flint, D. (1979), 'True and fair and ED24: directors' and auditor's dilemma', *Accountant's Magazine*, October.

Flint, D. (1980), *The Significance of the Standard True and Fair View*, New Zealand Society of Accountants.

Flint, D. (1982), *A True and Fair View in Company Accounts*, Institute of Chartered Accountants of Scotland.

Flint, D. (1984), 'A true and fair view: a UK perspective', in S.J. Gray and A.G. Coenenberg, *EEC Accounting Harmonisation*, North Holland.

Flint, D. (1988), 'A true and fair view in consolidated accounts' in S.J. Gray and A.G. Coenenberg, *International Group Accounting*, Croom Helm, 1988; 2nd edn Routledge, 1993.

Forster, A.A. (1983), 'The will o' the wisp of true and fair', *Professional Administrator*, January–March.

Fowle, M. (1992), 'True and fair – or only fairly true', *Accountancy*, June.

Gambling, T. (1970), 'True and fair view – fact or fiction?', *Accountancy*, March.

Gill, G.S. (1983), 'True and fair view', *Australian Accountant*, November.

Grace, E. (1988), 'Clearly spelling out the true and fair view', *Accountancy Age*, 30 June.

Graham, J. (1969), 'Too much freedom', *Accountancy*, November.

Griffiths, I. (1986), 'True and fairy tale', *Accountancy*, September.

Grinyer, J. (1984), 'True and fair – time for the ASC to act', *Accountant's Magazine*, January.

Gwilliam, D. and Russell, T. (1991), 'Compliance with the letter but not the spirit', *Accountancy*, April.

Harris, A.C. and Wilson, S.J. (1982), 'One audit opinion or two for CCA-1?', *Accountants' Journal* (NZ), May.

Harris, N.G.E. (1987), 'Fairness in financial reporting', *Journal of Applied Philosophy*, vol. 4, no. 1.

Hatherly, D.J. and Skuse, P.C.B. (1985), 'Audit reports', in D. Kent *et al.*, *Current Issues in Auditing*, Harper and Row.

Heazlewood, C.T. (1971), 'True and fair and the Companies (Amendment) Bill 1970', *Chartered Accountant in Australia*, April.

Higson, A. and Blake, J. (1993), 'The true and fair concept – a formula for international disharmony: some empirical evidence', *International Journal of Accounting*, vol., 28, no. 2.

Hines, R.D. (1987), 'Financial accounting standard setting: from truth to due process', *Chartered Accountant in Australia*, July.

Hoffman, L. and Arden, M.H. (1983), 'Legal opinion on true and fair', *Accountancy*, November.

Hope, J.A.D. (1984), 'True and fair: the opinion of Scottish Counsel', *Accountant's Magazine*, February.

Horrocks, J. (1967), 'Are published balance sheets untrue and unfair?', *Australian Accountant*, October.

Houghton, K.A. (1987), 'True and fair view: an empirical study of connotative meaning', *Accounting, Organizations and Society*, vol. 12, no. 2.

Hurst, K. (1993), 'Small companies: no longer true and fair?', *Accountancy*, May.

Jack, R.B. (1977), 'A lawyer looks at CCA-1', *Accountant's Magazine*, March.

Jackson, K. (1986), 'A true and fair and different view', *Accountancy*, October.

Johnston, T.R. (1967), 'Is the standard "true and fair view of the state of affairs" attainable in a balance sheet?', *Accountants' Journal* (NZ), July.

Jones, R. (1993), 'True and fair gymnastics', *Accountancy*, December.

Kenley, J., 'True and fair rules – some Australian observations', *Accountant's Magazine*, March.

Kenley, J. (1985), 'More from Australia on true and fair', *Accountant's Magazine*, February.

Kettle, R. (1950), 'Balance sheets and accounts under the Companies Act, 1948', in Baxter, W.T. (ed.), *Studies in Accounting*, Sweet & Maxwell.

Knox, J. and Duff, J. (1991), 'True, fair or false?', *Accountancy*, December.

Krishnan, V. (1991), 'Accrual basis *vis-à-vis* true and fair view', *Chartered Accountant* (India), May.

Lasok, K.P.E. and Grace, E. (1988), 'Fair accounting', *Journal of Business Law*, May.

Lasok, K.P.E. and Grace, E. (1989), 'The true and fair view', *Company Lawyer*, January.

Lee, T.A. (1972), 'The concept of truth and fairness', *Company Auditing*, 2nd edn 1982, 3rd edn 1986, Van Nostrand Reinhold, ch. 6.

Lee, T.A. (1982), 'The will-o'-the-wisp of true and fair', *Accountant*, 15 July. (Review of Flint, 1982.)

Lee, T.A. (1984), 'ASC, CCA and a true and fair view', *Accountant's Magazine*, April.

Lyas, C. (1992), 'Accounting and language', in Mumford, M. and Peasnell, K.V. (eds), *Philosophical Pespectives in Accounting*, Routledge.

Mao, Sheng Chow (1988), 'What is true and fair?', *Singapore Accountant*, November.

McGee, A. (1991), 'The "true and fair view" debate: a study in the legal regulation of accounting', *Modern Law Review*, November.

McGee, R. (1991), 'New prospectus law focuses on true and fair', *Accountant*, March.

McGregor, W. (1992), 'True and fair – an accounting anachronism', *Australian Accountant*, February.

Macve, R. and Jackson, J. (1991), *Marking to Market: Accounting for Marketable Securities in the Financial Services Industry*, Research Board of the Institute of·Chartered Accountants in England and Wales, ch. 3.

Miller, M.C. (1969), '"True and fair" and auditors' reports', *Australian Accountant*, April.

Mynors, P. (1992), 'In fairness and truth', *ReActions*, November.

Ng, A. Chew (1984), 'True and fair – an Australian overview', *Chartered Accountant* (India), September.

New Zealand Society of Accountants (1978), 'A true and fair view, Section 153(1) of the Companies Act, 1955', *Accountants' Journal* (NZ), February.

Nobes, C.W. (1993), 'The true and fair view requirement: impact on and of the Fourth Directive', *Accounting and Business Research*, Winter.

Nobes, C.W. and Parker, R.H. (1991), 'True and fair: a survey of UK financial directors', *Journal of Business Finance and Accounting*, Spring.

Ordelheide, D. (1993), 'True and fair view – a European and a German perspective. A commentary on 'A European true and fair view?' by David Alexander', *European Accounting Review*, May.

Parker, R.H. (1989), 'Importing and exporting accounting: the British experience', in Hopwood, A.G. (ed.), *International Pressures for Accounting Change*, Prentice-Hall International.

Parker, R.H. and Nobes, C.W. (1991), 'Auditors' view of true and fair', *Accounting and Business Research*, Autumn.

Pawson, P. (1987), 'A matter of balance sheet presentation', *Accountancy*, January.

Pham, D. (1984), 'A true and fair view: a French perspective', in S.J. Gray and A.G. Coenenberg, *EEC Accounting Harmonisation*, North Holland.

Popoff, B. (1983), 'Some conceptualizing on the true and fair view', *International Journal of Accounting*, Fall.

Pound, G.D. (1985), 'True and fair debate – accounting bodies reply', *Chartered Accountant in Australia*, March.

Reynolds, P. (1984), 'Can the balance sheet be seen to be true and fair?', *Accountant's Magazine*, September.

Richardson, J.P.C. (1966), 'A true and fair view seen from the United States', *Accountancy*, October.

Riley, B.B. (1973), 'Directors and accounting principles – quo vadis', *Chartered Accountant in Australia*, June.

Rutherford, B. (1983), 'Spoilt beauty: the true and fair doctrine in translation', *AUTA Review*, Spring.

Rutherford, B.A. (1985), 'The true and fair view doctrine: a search for explication', *Journal of Business Finance and Accounting*, Winter.

Rutherford, B.A. (1988), 'The explication of the true and fair view doctrine: a reply', *Journal of Business Finance and Accounting*, Spring.

Rutherford, B.A. (1989), 'The true and fair view doctrine: some recent developments', in Macdonald, G. and Rutherford, B.A. (eds), *Accounts, Accounting and Accountability*, Van Nostrand Reinhold.

Ryan, F.J.O. (1967), 'A true and fair view', *Abacus*, December.

Ryan, F.J.O. (1974), 'A true and fair view revisited', *Australian Accountant*, February.

Ryan, J. (1985), 'A recipe for added confusion', *Australian Accountant*, September.

Ryan, J.B. (1980), 'A true and fair view: an accounting interpretation', in Emanuel, D. and Stewart, I., *Essays in Honour of Trevor R. Johnston*, University of Auckland Press.

Sadhu, M.A. and Langfield-Smith, I.A. (1993), *A Qualitative Standard for General Purpose Financial Reports: A Review*, Australian Accounting Research Foundation.

Shanahan, J. (1990), 'True and fair – what does it mean?', *Australian Business*, 31 January.

Shaw, J.C. (1979), 'The audit response to ED24 – the case for review without report', *Accountant's Magazine*, August.

Smart, C. (1985), 'Life company accounts distorting the true picture', *Accountancy*, March.

South African Chartered Accountant (1972), 'Fare thee well true-and-fair?', August.

Steele, A. and Haworth, J. (1986), 'Auditor's views on truth and fairness of CCA', *Accounting and Business Research*, Spring.

Stewart, I.C. (1988), 'The explication of the true and fair view doctrine: a comment', *Journal of Business Finance and Accounting*, Spring.

Stobart, P. (1989), 'Brand valuation: a true and fair view', *Accountancy*, October.

Sugden, A. (1989), 'Public relations: the conflict with true and fair', *Accountancy*, September.

Sykes, T. (1990), 'True, fair or false?', *Australian Business*, 4 July.

Tilly, H.S.J. (1982), 'Two audit opinions better than one?', *Accountants' Journal* (NZ), August.

Tweedie, D.P. (1983), 'True and fair rules', *Accountant's Magazine*, November.

Tweedie, D. (1988), 'True and fair v. the rule book: which is the answer to creative accounting?', *Pacific Accounting Review*, December.

Tweedie, D. and Kellas, J. (1987), 'Off-balance sheet financing', *Accountancy*, April.

Tweedie, D. and Kellas, J. (1988), 'Setting the accountants' record straight', *Accountancy*, January.

Urgent Issues Task Force (1992), 'Abstract 7. True and fair view override disclosures', reprinted in *Accountancy*, February 1993.

Van Hulle, K. (1993), 'Truth and untruth about true and fair: a commentary on "A European true and fair view?"', *European Accounting Review*, May.

[Walker, R.G.] (1984), *'A True and Fair View' and the Reporting Obligations of Directors and Auditors*, National Companies and Securities Commission.

Walker, R.G. (1986), 'True and fair view revisited', *Australian Accountant*, April.

Walker, R.G. (1992), 'Let's redefine – not dump – true and fair view', *New Accountant*, 15 October.

Waller, D. (1990), 'Time to get rid of true and fair', *Accountant's Magazine*, December.

Walton, P. (1991), *The True and Fair View: A Shifting Concept*, Occasional Research Paper No. 7, Chartered Association of Certified Accountants.

Walton, P. (1993), 'Introduction: the true and fair view in British accounting', *European Accounting Review*, May.

Whewell, R. (1990), 'Accounting for life assurance: truly fair or fairly true?', *Accountancy*, February.

Whitely, C. (1988), 'ED42: central to the concept of true and fair', *Accountancy*, April.

Wild, K. (1987), 'Off-balance sheet finance – why all the fuss?', *Accountancy*, June.

Williams, D.W. (1985), 'Legal perspectives on auditing', in D. Kent *et al.*, *Current Issues in Auditing*, Harper & Row.

Wolnizer, P.W. (1985), '"Correspondence with the facts" – a recurrent theme in commentaries on the statutory quality standard of truth and fairness in accounts', *Company and Securities Law Journal*, August.

Woolf, E. (1986), 'Users of accounts want more than just true and fair', *Accountancy*, January.

Zeff, S.A. (1990), 'The English-language equivalent of *Geeft een Getrouw Beeld*', *De Accountant*, October.

Zeff, S.A., van der Wel, F. and Camfferman, K. (1992), *Company Financial Reporting: A Historical and Comparative Study of the Dutch Regulatory Process*, North Holland, ch. 3.

Appendices

Appendix I

'The English-language equivalent of *Geeft een Getrouw Beeld*' by Stephen A. Zeff (1990)

It has been the practice of Dutch auditing firms to translate '*geeft een getrouw beeld*' as either 'present fairly' (American usage) or 'give a true and fair view' (British usage), largely depending on the wishes of the client or the predisposition of the auditor. Major auditing firms are known to use one translation for some clients, and the other translation for others. No guidance has been issued by the Nederlands Instituut van Registeraccountants, probably in the belief that the two translations mean the same thing, and that the issue is unimportant. In fact, the issue is not unimportant, as the two translations do not mean the same thing.

In the United States, the key phrase that appears in all auditors' reports is 'present fairly . . . in conformity with generally accepted accounting principles'. Since the first usage of the language in the 1930s 'present fairly' has always been linked with 'generally accepted accounting principles'. The practical meaning of the passage is that, since the company's financial statements have been prepared in conformity with generally accepted accounting principles, they necessarily 'present fairly'. Hardly any cases are known in which American auditors have reported that, in their opinion, the financial statements 'present fairly' notwithstanding one or more material departures from generally accepted accounting principles.

Indeed, in 1978 the Commission on Auditors' Responsibilities, which had been created by the American Institute of Certified Public Accountants (AICPA) recommended that the term 'fairly' be deleted from the standard form of the auditor's report. The Commission's belief was that 'fairly' is subject to misinterpretation and, furthermore, it is redundant. The critical consideration is, in all cases, whether generally accepted accounting principles have been followed. Two years later, the AICPA's Auditing Standards Board actually proposed, in an exposure draft, that 'fairly' be deleted from the standard form of the auditor's report. After receiving some negative reactions in letters of comment, the Board decided not to press the matter further. Nonetheless, one can hardly escape the conclusion that 'present fairly' is not a vital element in the American auditor's report in the opinion of at least some leaders of the profession.

In the United Kingdom, by contrast, 'give a true and fair view' stands on its own as the indispensable element in the auditor's opinion on the financial statements. The phrase has been part of the UK Companies Act since 1947, while 'present fairly' does not possess comparable legal standing in the United States. Hence, if a Dutch auditor seeks to translate '*geeft een getrouw beeld*' into an equivalent phrase in the English language, the proper choice would be 'give a true and fair view'. In the UK, one talks of the 'true and fair override', since this quality governs any disputes over proper practice. In the Netherlands, '*getrouw beeld*' is, according to the recommendation issued by the NIVRA Council, the quality, standing alone, upon which the auditor is to give an opinion.

A historical argument may also be introduced to justify 'give a true and fair view' as the proper English translation of '*geeft een getrouw beeld*'. In the deliberations of the Groupe d'Etudes over the Fourth Directive of the European Community, the initial position reflected the German preference for conformity with the law. Once the UK joined the Community in 1973, British members of the Groupe d'Etudes argued successfully in favour of a subjective criterion based on the auditor's judgment, rather than on conformity with the law. In the official English-language translation of the Fourth Directive, 'true and fair view' appears in Section 1, Article 2. This would be the English equivalent of, as examples, the French '*image fidèle*' or the German '*getreues Bild*'.

While it is true that '*getrouw*' has appeared in Dutch statute law (currently in Article 362, paragraph 2 of Title 9 of Book 2 of the Civil Code) since 1970, the Memorie van Toelichting refers only to the British equivalent: '*Historisch is de uitdrukking "getrouw" op te vatten als het resultaat van een poging de Engelse uitdrukking "true and fair" in het Nederlands te vertalen*'.

My argument is that the American and UK auditing professions do not use the terms 'present fairly' and 'give a true and fair view' equivalently. In fact, the term 'present fairly', standing alone, is *never* seen in American auditors' reports. Its meaning is directly dependent on 'generally accepted accounting principles', which is defined by reference to a large body of authoritative literature.

In contrast, '*in het maatschappelijk verkeer als aanvaardbaar worden beschouwd*' lacks a comparable authoritative literature. In my view, Dutch auditing firms should translate '*geeft een getrouw beeld*' as 'give a true and fair view'. This practice would promote comparability in the European Community and it would adopt a terminology that possesses an equivalent meaning to '*een getrouw beeld*', which is the quality of the auditor's judgment.

If the proposed reform of the Dutch auditor's report, as set out in the *Ontwerp-Richtlijn* dated 15 September 1989, goes into effect, the opinion paragraph of the unqualified auditor's report would become virtually identical to the UK report, since the latter refers both to whether the accounts 'give a true and fair view' and to whether they 'have been properly prepared in accordance with' company law. Hence, the argument advanced above would be even stronger.

This paper first appeared in the October 1990 issue of De Accountant. *We are grateful to Steve Zeff and to the editor of the journal for allowing us to reprint the article.*

Appendix II

The Opinion of English Counsel (then known as Leonard Hoffman QC and Mary Arden) on true and fair (1983)

1. The Accounting Standards Committee ('ASC') from time to time issues Statements of Standard Accounting Practice ('SSAPs'). These are declared in the Explanatory Foreword to be 'methods of accounting approved ... for application to all financial accounts intended to give a true and fair view of financial position and profit and loss'. They are not intended to be 'a comprehensive code of rigid rules' but departures from them should be disclosed and explained. The Committee also noted in its Explanatory Foreword that 'methods of financial accounting evolve and alter in response to changing business and economic needs. From time to time new accounting standards will be drawn at progressive levels, and established standards will be reviewed with the object of improvement in the light of new needs and developments.'

2. The ASC has recently undertaken a review of the standard setting process and decided that future standards will 'deal only with those matters which are of major and fundamental importance and affect the generality of companies' but that, as in the past, the standards will apply 'to all accounts which are intended to show a true and fair view of financial position and profit or loss'. A SSAP is therefore a declaration by the ASC, on behalf of its constituent professional bodies, that save in exceptional circumstances accounts which do not comply with the standard will not give a true and fair view.

3. But the preparation of accounts which give a true and fair view is not merely a matter of compliance with professional standards. In many important cases it is a requirement of law. Since 1947 all accounts prepared for the purpose of compliance with the Companies Acts have been required to 'give a true and fair view': s 13(1) of the Companies Act 1947, re-enacted as s 149(1) of the Companies Act 1948. In 1978 the concept of a true and fair view was adopted by the EEC Council in its Fourth Directive 'on the annual accounts of certain types of

companies'. The Directive combined the requirement of giving a true and fair view with extremely detailed provisions about the form and contents of the accounts but the obligation to give a true and fair view was declared to be overriding. Accounts must not comply with the detailed requirements if this would prevent them from giving a true and fair view. Parliament gave effect to the Directive by passing the Companies Act 1981. This substitutes a new section 149(2) in the 1948 Act, reproducing the old section 149(1) in substantially similar words. The detailed requirements of the Directive appear as a new Eighth Schedule to the 1948 Act. The old section 149(1) (now renumbered 149a(1)) and the old Eighth Schedule (now Schedule 8A) are retained for the accounts of banking, insurance and shipping companies. So far as the requirement to give a true and fair view is concerned, a difference between 149(2) and 149A(1) is that the former has come into the law via Brussels whereas the latter has no EEC pedigree.

4. 'True and fair view' is thus a legal concept and the question of whether company accounts comply with section 149(2) (or section 149A(1)) can be authoritatively decided only by a court. This gives rise to a number of questions about the relationship between the legal requirement and the SSAPs issued by the ASC, which also claim to be authoritative statements on what is a true and fair view. What happens if there is a conflict between the professional standards demanded by the ASC and the decisions of the courts on the requirements of the Companies Act? Furthermore, the ASC issues new SSAPs 'at progressive levels' and reviews established ones. How is this consistent with a statutory requirement of a true and fair view which has been embodied in the law in the same language since 1947? Can the issue of a new SSAP make it unlawful to prepare accounts in a form which would previously have been lawful? How can the ASC have power to legislate in this way?

5. To answer these questions it is necessary first to examine the nature of the 'true and fair view' concept as used in the Companies Act. It is an abstraction or philosophical concept expressed in simple English. The law uses many similar concepts, of which 'reasonable care' is perhaps the most familiar example. It is a common feature of such concepts that there is seldom any difficulty in understanding what they mean but frequent controversy over their application to particular facts. One reason for this phenomenon is that because such concepts represent a very high level of abstraction which has to be applied to an infinite variety of concrete facts, there can never be a sharply defined line between, for example, what is reasonable care and what is not. There will always be a penumbral area in which views may reasonably differ.

6. The courts have never attempted to define 'true and fair' in the sense of offering a paraphrase in other language and in our opinion have been wise not to do so. When a concept can be expressed in ordinary English words, we do not think that it illuminates their meaning to attempt to frame a definition. We doubt, for example, whether the man on the Clapham omnibus has really contributed very much to the understanding of reasonable care or that accountants have found it helpful to ask themselves how this imaginary passenger would have prepared a set of accounts. It is much more useful to illustrate the concept in action, for example, to explain why certain accounts do or do not give a true and fair view.

7. It is however important to observe that the application of the concept involves judgment in questions of degree. The information contained in accounts must be accurate and comprehensive (to mention two of the most obvious elements which contribute to a true and fair view) to within acceptable limits. What is acceptable and how is this to be achieved? Reasonable businessmen and accountants may differ over the degree of accuracy or comprehensiveness which in particular cases the accounts should attain. Equally, there may sometimes be room for differences over the method to adopt in order to give a true and fair view, cases in which there may be more than one 'true and fair view' of the same financial position. Again, because 'true and fair view' involves questions of degree, we think that cost-effectiveness must play a part in deciding the amount of information which is sufficient to make accounts true and fair.

8. In the end, as we have said, the question of whether accounts give a true and fair view in compliance with the Companies Acts must be decided by a judge. But the courts look for guidance on this question to the ordinary practices of professional accountants. This is not merely because accounts are expressed in a language which judges find difficult to understand. This may sometimes be true but it is a minor reason for the importance which the courts attach to evidence of accountancy practice. The important reason is inherent in the nature of the 'true and fair' concept. Accounts will not be true and fair unless the information they contain is sufficient in quantity and quality to satisfy the reasonable expectations of the readers to whom they are addressed. On this question, accountants can express an informed professional opinion on what, in current cicumstances, it is thought that accounts should reasonably contain. But they can do more than that. The readership of accounts will consist of businessmen, investors, bankers and so forth, as well as professional accountants. But the expectations of the readers will have been moulded by the practices of accountants because by and large

they will expect to get what they ordinarily get and that in turn will depend upon the normal practices of accountants.

9. For these reasons, the courts will treat compliance with accepted accounting principles as prima facie evidence that the accounts are true and fair. Equally, deviation from accepted principles will be prima facie evidence that they are not. We have not been able to find reported cases on the specific question of whether accounts are true and fair, although the question has been adverted to in the course of judgments on other matters; see for example *Willingdale v International Commercial Bank Ltd* [1978] AC 834. There are however some cases on the analogous question arising in income tax cases of whether profit or loss has been calculated in accordance with 'the correct principles of commercial accountancy' and there is a helpful statement of principle (approved in subsequent cases in the Court of Appeal) by Pennycuick V-C in *Odeon Associated Theatres Ltd* [1971] 1 WLR 442 at 454:–

> In order to ascertain what are the correct principles [the court] has recourse to the evidence of accountants. That evidence is conclusive on the practice of accountants in the sense of the principles on which accountants act in practice. That is a question of pure fact, but the court itself has to make a final decision as to whether that practice corresponds to the correct principles of commercial accountancy. No doubt in the vast proportion of cases the court will agree with the accountants but it will not necessarily do so. Again, there may be a divergency of views between the accountants, or there may be alternative principles, none of which can be said to be incorrect, or of course there may be no accountancy evidence at all. . . . At the end of the day the court must determine what is the correct principle of commercial accountancy to be applied.

10. This is also in our opinion the relationship between generally accepted accounting principles and the legal concept of 'true and fair'. The function of the ASC is to formulate what it considers should be generally accepted accounting principles. Thus the value of a SSAP to a court which has to decide whether accounts are true and fair is two-fold. First, it represents an important statement of professional opinion about the standards which readers may reasonably expect in accounts which are intended to be true and fair. The SSAP is intended to crystallise professional opinion and reduce penumbral areas in which divergent practices exist and can each have a claim to being 'true and fair'. Secondly, because accountants are professionally obliged to comply with a SSAP, it creates in the readers an expectation that the accounts will be in conformity with the prescribed

standards. This is in itself a reason why accounts which depart from the standard without adequate justification or explanation may be held not to be true and fair. The importance of expectations was emphasised by the Court of Appeal in what may be regarded as a converse case, *Re Press Caps* [1949] Ch 434. An ordinary historic cost balance sheet was said to be 'true and fair' notwithstanding that it gave no information about the current value of freehold properties because, it was said, no one familiar with accounting conventions would expect it to include such information.

11. A SSAP therefore has no direct legal effect. It is simply a rule of professional conduct for accountants. But in our opinion it is likely to have an indirect effect on the content which the courts will give to the 'true and fair' concept. The effect of a SSAP may therefore be to make it likely that accounts which would previously have been considered true and fair will no longer satisfy the law. Perhaps the most dramatic example arises out of the recent statement by the ASC in connection with its review of SSAP 16 'Current Cost Accounting'. The Statement puts forward for discussion the proposition that 'where a company is materially affected by changing prices, pure HC accounts do not give a true and fair view'. If this proposition were embodied in a new SSAP and accepted by the courts, the legal requirements of a true and fair view will have undergone a revolutionary change.

12. There is no inconsistency between such a change brought about by changing professional opinion and the rule that words in a statute must be construed in accordance with the meaning which they bore when the statute was passed. The *meaning* of true and fair remains what it was in 1947. It is the *content* given to the concept which has changed. This is something which constantly happens to such concepts. For example, the Bill of Rights 1688 prohibited 'cruel and unusual punishments'. There has been no change in the meaning of 'cruel' since 1688. The definition in Dr Johnson's Dictionary of 1755 ('pleased with hurting others, inhuman, hardhearted, without pity, barbarous') is much the same as in a modern dictionary. But changes in society mean that a judge in 1983 would unquestionably characterise punishments as 'cruel' which his predecessor of 1688 would not have thought to come within this description. The meaning of the concept remains the same; the facts to which it is applied have changed.

13. The possibility of changing accounting standards has been recognised both by the courts and the legislature. In *Associated Portland Cement Maufacturers Ltd v Price Commission* [1975] ICR 27, esp at 45-6, the court recognised changes since 1945 in the permissible methods of calculating depreciation. Similarly paragraph 90 of the new Eighth

Schedule to the Companies Act 1948 refers to 'principles generally accepted . . . at the time when those accounts are prepared'.

14. We therefore see no conflict between the functions of the ASC in formulating standards which it declares to be essential to true and fair accounts and the function of the courts in deciding whether the accounts satisfy the law. The courts are of course not bound by a SSAP. A court may say that accounts which ignore them are nevertheless true and fair. But the immediate effect of a SSAP is to strengthen the likelihood that a court will hold that compliance with the prescribed standard is necessary for the accounts to give a true and fair view. In the absence of a SSAP, a court is unlikely to reject accounts drawn up in accordance with principles which command some respectable professional support. The issue of a SSAP has the effect, for the two reasons which we have given in paragraph 10, of creating a prima facie presumption that accounts which do not comply are not true and fair. This presumption is then strengthened or weakened by the extent to which the SSAP is actually accepted and applied. Universal acceptance means that it is highly unlikely that a court would accept accounts drawn up according to different principles. On the other hand, if there remains a strong body of professional opinion which consistently opts out of applying the SSAP, giving reasons which the ASC may consider inadequate, the prima facie presumption against such accounts is weakened.

15. We therefore do not think that the ASC should be concerned by the possibility that a court may hold that compliance with one of its SSAPs is not necessary for the purposes of the Companies Acts. This possibility is inherent in the fact that the courts are not bound by professional opinion. The function of the ASC is to express their professional judgment on the standards which in their opinion are required.

16. There are two further points to be considered. The first is the relationship between the 'true and fair' requirement and the detailed provisions of the new Eighth Schedule. The Act is quite explicit on this point: the true and fair view is overriding. Nevertheless it may be said that the detailed requirements offer some guidance as to the principles which Parliament considered would give a true and fair view. In particular, the Schedule plainly regards historic cost accounting as the norm and current cost accounting as an optional alternative. In these circumstances, is a court likely to follow a SSAP which declares that for certain companies, historic cost accounts *cannot* give a true and fair view? In our opinion, whatever reasons there may be for taking one view or the other, the provisions of the Eighth Schedule are no obstacle to accepting such a SSAP. As we have already pointed out, the

the provisions of the Schedule are static whereas the concept of a true and fair view is dynamic. If the latter is overriding, it is not impossible that the effect in time will be to render obsolete some of the provisions of the Schedule. But we think that this is what must have been intended when overriding force was given to a concept with a changing content.

17. Lastly, there is the effect of the adoption of 'true and fair view' by the EEC. Because section 149(2) of the 1948 Act now gives effect to a Directive, it must (unlike section 149A(1)) be construed in accordance with any decision of the European Court on the meaning of Article 2.3 of the Directive. In practice we do not think that this is likely to affect the evolution of the concept in England. Just as the concept may have a different content at different times, so it may have a different content in different countries. Although the European Court may seek to achieve some uniformity by laying down minimum standards for the accounts of all EEC countries, it seems to us that they are unlikely to disapprove of higher standards being required by the professional bodies of individual states and in consequence, higher legal criteria for what is a true and fair view being adopted in the national courts of some member states.

18. So for example Article 33 of the Directive gives member states the right to 'permit or require' companies to use current cost accounting instead of historic cost principles. In the UK, as we have said, current cost accounts are permitted by the Eighth Schedule but the only circumstances in which they may be required is if a court should decide, on the basis of prevailing principles, that they were necessary to give a true and fair view. In Germany, on the other hand, the equivalent of the Eighth Schedule does not even permit current cost accounts. In Germany, therefore, the only way they could be permitted would be if the German court applied 'true and fair view' as an overriding requirement. For the reasons given in paragraph 16, we do not regard it as illogical or impossible that even a German court may take this view. But having regard to the Directive, we think it is very unlikely that the European Court would decide as a matter of community law that there are circumstances in which historic cost accounts do not give a true and fair view. Developments of this kind are more likely to be left to national courts to make in the light of local professional opinion.

This opinion was first published in Accountancy, *November 1983.*

Appendix III

The Opinion of Scottish Counsel (then known as J.A.D. Hope) on true and fair (1984)

In their Opinion, English Counsel examine the nature of the 'true and fair view' concept as used in the Companies Acts in some detail. They draw attention to the fact that the Courts have never attempted to define this term, in the sense of offering a paraphrase of it, and go on to say that the application of the concept involves judgment in questions of degree. Turning to the relationship between the legal concept of 'true and fair' on the one hand and generally accepted accounting principles on the other, they say that the Courts will treat compliance with accepted accounting principles as prima facie evidence that the accounts are true and fair, and that equally deviation from accepted principles will be prima facie evidence that they are not. This leads them to consider the problem of the effect upon the 'true and fair view' concept of a new Statement of Standard Accounting Practice ('SSAP'). Their answer to it is to say that there is no inconsistency between a change in the legal requirements for a true and fair view resulting from a new SSAP and the rule that words in a statute must be construed in accordance with the meaning which they bore when the statute was passed. As they put it, 'The *meaning* of true and fair remains what it was in 1947. It is the *content* given to the concept which has changed.' Thus the concept of the 'true and fair view' is, they say, dynamic, with a changing content as accounting practices are revised and developed with time. The importance of this conclusion is revealed when they recognise, in paragraph 16 of their Opinion, that since the 'true and fair' view requirement in section 149(2) of the Companies Act 1948 as amended overrides the provisions of the new Schedule 8 to the Act, it may have the effect in time of rendering obsolete some of the detailed provisions of the Schedule.

Had I been approaching the matter afresh I would have reached the same conclusions as English Counsel have done, for substantially the same reasons. While the various authorities to which they refer in the course of their discussion are cases decided in the English Courts, the principles upon which their opinion is based are all familiar to a Scottish lawyer, and the statutes are of course applicable with equal force in both countries. It is equally true of Scotland to say that the Courts have not attempted to provide a definition of the term 'true and fair view', although there have been a number of recent cases where the sufficiency of a company's accounts in that regard has come under consideration. In each case the question whether or not they present a 'true and fair view' is a question of fact, which the Court will decide in the light of the evidence, including evidence of current accounting practice. As in England, the court is likely to pay close attention to the evidence of accountants without feeling bound by that evidence: cf, *Lord Advocate v Ruffle*, 1979 SC 351. The statement of principle by Pennycuick V-C in *Odeon Associated Theatres v Jones* (1971) 1 WLR 442 at p 454, which English Counsel quote in paragraph 9 of their Opinion, as explained by Lord Denning, MR, in *Heather v PE Consulting Group Limited* (1973) Ch 189, is familiar in this country, and has been referred to in the Scottish Court on a number of occasions, particularly in tax cases.

The distinction which English Counsel draw between the meaning of the term 'true and fair' on the one hand and its content on the other is entirely sound in my opinion. This is because the answer to the question whether a true and fair view is given by the accounts inevitably involves questions of fact and degree, which must always be decided by reference to the state of affairs generally at the time when the accounts were prepared. An analogy can be drawn with other concepts used by the law, such as 'reasonable care' and 'reasonably practicable'. The latter expression, for instance, is used in a variety of provisions to be found in the Factories Act 1961 and its subordinate legislation. The meaning of the phrase, no doubt, must be taken to have remained the same since the date of the enactment, but it is well established in Scotland as well as in England that, when it comes to considering whether in any particular case measures which might have been taken so as to avoid the accident were or were not reasonably practicable, regard must be had to the state of current knowledge and invention. In my opinion an argument to the effect that the question whether a particular set of accounts gave a true and fair view had to be decided with reference to principles of accounting which, while current in 1947 or 1948, had become obsolete by the time the accounts were prepared only has to be stated to be seen to be unacceptable. I agree with English Counsel that it is reasonable to think that the reason why overriding force was given by the Companies Act 1981 to the concept of the 'true and fair view' is that it was recognised that this was a dynamic concept with a changing content, capable of rendering obsolete any particular provision in the Schedule which had become inconsistent with current practice.

For these reasons I am of the opinion that the guidance which English Counsel have given to the Accounting Standards Committee can be accepted as being in accordance with the Scottish approach.

This Opinion was first published in Accountant's Magazine, *February 1984.*

Appendix IV
The up-dated Opinion of English Counsel (Mary Arden QC) on true and fair (21 April 1993)

1. This Opinion is concerned with the effect of recent changes in the law on the relationship between accounting standards and the requirement in Sections 226 and 227 of the Companies Act 1985 (as amended) that accounts drawn up in accordance with the Companies Act 1985 give a true and fair view of the state of affairs of the company, and where applicable the group, at the end of the financial year in question and of the profit or loss of the Company or group for that financial year. (I shall call this requirement 'the true and fair requirement'). As is well known, the true and fair requirement is overriding. Thus both sections provide that where in special circumstances compliance with the requirements of the Act as to the matters to be included in the accounts would be inconsistent with the true and fair requirement there must be a departure from those requirements to the extent necessary to give true and fair view (sections 226(5) and 227(6)). The meaning of the true and fair requirement, as it appeared in earlier legislation, was discussed in detail in the joint Opinions which I wrote in 1983 and 1984 with Leonard Hoffmann QC (now the Right Hon Lord Justice Hoffmann).

2. As stated in those Opinions, the question whether accounts satisfy the true and fair requirement is a question of law for the Court. However, while the true and fair view which the law requires to be given is not qualified in any way, the task of interpreting the true and fair requirement cannot be performed by the Court without evidence as to the practices and views of accountants. The more authoritative those practices and views, the more ready the Court will be to follow them. Those practices and views do not of course stand still. They respond to such matters as advances in accounting and changes in the economic climate and business practice. The law will not prevent the proper development of the practices and views of accountants but rather, through the process of interpretation, will reflect such development.

3. Up to August 1990 the responsibility for developing accounting standards was discharged by the Accounting Standards Committee ('the ASC'). Since August 1990 that responsibility has been discharged by the Accounting Standards Board ('the Board'). The 'Foreword to Accounting Standards' approved by the Board describes in particular the circumstances in which accounts are expected to comply with accounting standards. For this purpose the key paragraph is paragraph 16, which provides

> Accounting standards are authoritative statements of how particular types of transaction and other events should be reflected in financial statements and accordingly compliance with accounting standards will normally be necessary for financial statements to give a true and fair view.

The Foreword also describes the extensive process of investigation and consultation which precedes the issue of a standard and explains that the major accountancy bodies expect their members to observe accounting standards and may enquire into apparent failures by their members to observe standards or ensure adequate disclosure of departures from them.

4. What is the role of an accounting standard? The initial purpose is to identify proper accounting practice for the benefit of preparers and auditors of accounts. However, because accounts commonly comply with accounting standards, the effect of the issue of standards has also been to create a common understanding between users and preparers of accounts as to how particular items should be treated in accounts and accordingly an expectation that save where good reason exists accounts will comply with applicable accounting standards.

5. The Companies Act 1989 now gives statutory recognition to the existence of accounting standards and by implication to their beneficial role in financial reporting. This recognition is achieved principally through the insertion of a new section (Section 256) into the Companies Act 1985 and of a new disclosure requirement into Schedule 4 to that Act. Section 256 provides:

(1) In this Part 'accounting standards' means statements of standard accounting practice issued by such body or bodies as may be prescribed by regulations.

(2) References in this Part to accounting standards applicable to a company's annual accounts are to such standards as are, in accordance with their terms, relevant to the company's circumstances and to the accounts.

(3) The Secretary of State may make grants to or for the purposes of bodies concerned with:

   (a) issuing accounting standards,
   (b) overseeing and directing the issuing of such standards, or
   (c) investigating departures from such standards or from the accounting requirements of this Act and taking steps to secure compliance with them.

(4) Regulations under this section may contain such transitional and other supplementary and incidental provisions as appear to the Secretary of State to be appropriate.

In addition the notes to financial statements prepared under Schedule 4 must now comply with the following new requirement:* '36A. It shall be stated whether the accounts have been prepared in accordance with applicable accounting standards and particulars of any material departure from those standards and the reasons for it shall be given.'

6. Another significant change brought about by the 1989 Act is the introduction of a procedure whereby the Secretary of State or a person authorised by him may ask the Court to determine whether annual accounts comply with inter alia the true and fair requirement (Section 245B of the Companies Act 1985). The Financial Reporting Review Panel ('the Review Panel') has been authorised by the Secretary of State for this purpose. By agreement with the Department of Trade and Industry the ambit of the Review Panel is normally public and large private companies, with the Department exercising its powers in other cases.

7. The changes brought about by the Companies Act 1989 will in my view affect the way in which the Court approaches the question whether compliance with an accounting standard is necessary to satisfy the true and fair view requirement. The Court will infer from Section 256 that statutory policy favours both the issue of accounting standards (by a body prescribed by regulation) and compliance with them: indeed Section 256(3)(c) additionally contemplates the investigation of departures from them and confers power to provide public funding for such purpose. The Court will also in my view infer from paragraph 36A of Schedule 4 that (since the requirement is to disclose particulars of non-compliance rather than of compliance) accounts which meet the true and fair requirement will in general follow rather than depart from standards and that departure is sufficiently abnormal to require to be justified. These factors increase the likelihood, to which the earlier joint Opinions referred, that the Courts will hold that in general compliance with accounting standards is necessary to meet the true and fair requirement.

8. The status of accounting standards in legal proceedings has also in my view been enhanced by the changes in the standard-setting process since 1989. Prior to the Companies Act 1989 accounting standards were developed by the ASC, which was a committee established by the six professional accountancy bodies who form the Consultative Committee of Accountancy Bodies ('the CCAB') and funded by them. The standard-setting process was reviewed by a committee established by the CCAB under the chairmanship of Sir Ron Dearing CB. The report of that Committee (the Dearing Report), which was published in 1988 and is entitled *The Making of Accounting Standards*, contained a number of recommendations, including recommendations leading to what are now paragraph 36A and Section 245B and the further recommendation that the standard-setting body should be funded on a wider basis. As a result of the implementation of these recommendations the standard-setting body no longer represents simply the views of the accountancy profession. Its members are appointed by a committee drawn from the Council of the Financial Reporting Council Limited ('the FRC'). The Council includes representatives of the Government, representatives of the business and financial community and members of the accountancy profession. Moreover, the Board is now funded, via the FRC, jointly by the Government, the financial community and the accountancy profession.

9. The statements referred to in Section 256 are of *standard* accounting practice. Parliament has thus recognised the desirability of standardisation in the accountancy field. The discretion to determine the measure of standardisation is one of the matters left to the Board. By definition, standardisation may restrict the availability of particular accounting treatments. Moreover the Act does not require that the practices required by a standard should necessarily be those prevailing or generally accepted at the time.

10. As explained in the earlier Joint Opinions in relation to statements of standard accounting practice, the immediate effect of the issue of an accounting standard is to create a likelihood that the court will hold that compliance with that standard is necessary to meet the true and fair requirement. That likelihood is strengthened by the degree to which a standard is subsequently accepted in practice. Thus if a particular standard is generally followed, the court is very likely to find that accounts must comply with it in order to show a true and fair view. The converse of that proposition, that non-acceptance of a standard in practice would almost inevitably lead a court to the conclusion that compliance with it was not necessary to meet the true and fair requirement, is not however, the case. Whenever a standard is issued by the Board, then, irrespective

of the lack in some quarters of support for it, the court would be bound to give special weight to the opinion of the Board in view of its status as the standard-setting body, the process of investigation, discussion and consultation that it will have undertaken before adopting the standard and the evolving nature of accounting standards.

11. The fact that paragraph 36A envisages the possibility of a departure from an 'applicable accounting standard' (in essence, any relevant standard: see section 256(2), above) does not mean that the Companies Act permits a departure in any case where the disclosure is given. The departure must have been appropriate in the particular case. If the Court is satisfied that compliance with a standard is necessary to show a true and fair view in that case, a departure will result in a breach of the true and fair requirement even if the paragraph 36A disclosure is given.

12. Experience shows that from time to time and for varying reasons deficiencies in accounting standards appear. Following a recommendation in the Dearing Report, the Board has established a sub-committee called the Urgent Issues Task Force ('the UITF') to resolve such issues on an urgent basis in appropriate cases. The members of the UITF include leading members of the accountancy profession and of the business community. The agenda of the UITF is published in advance to allow for public debate. The UITF's consensus pronouncements (contained in abstracts) represent the considered views of a large majority of its members. When the UITF reaches its view, it is considered by the Board for compliance with the law and accounting standards and with the Board's future plans. If an abstract meets these criteria the Board expects to adopt it without further consideration. It will then be published by the Board. The expectation of the CCAB, the Board and the profession is that abstracts of the UITF will be observed. This expectation has been borne out in practice. Accordingly in my view, the Court is likely to treat UITF abstracts as of considerable standing even though they are not envisaged by the Companies Acts. This will lead to a readiness on the part of the Court to accept that compliance with abstracts of the UITF is also necessary to meet the true and fair requirement.

13. The Joint Opinions were particularly concerned with the effect of standards on the concept of true and fair. The approach to standards taken in the Joint Opinions is consistent with the approach of the Court in *Lloyd Cheyham v Littlejohn* [1987] BCLC 303 at 313. In that case Woolf J. (as he then was) held that standards of the ASC were 'very strong evidence as to what is the proper standard which should be adopted'.

14. As regards the concept of true and fair, I would emphasize the point made in the joint Opinions that the true and fair view is a dynamic

concept. Thus what is required to show a true and fair view is subject to continuous rebirth and in determining whether the true and fair requirement is satisfied the Court will not in my·view seek to find synonyms for the words 'true' and 'fair' but will seek to apply the concepts which those words imply.

15. It is nearly a decade since the joint Opinions were written. Experience and legislative history since then have both illustrated the subtlety and evolving nature of the relationship between law and accounting practice. Accounting standards are now assured as an authoritative source of the latter. In consequence it is now the norm for accounts to comply with accounting standards. I would add this. Just as a custom which is upheld by the courts may properly be regarded as a source of law, so too, in my view, does an accounting standard which the court holds must be complied with to meet the true and fair requirement become, in cases where it is applicable, a source of law in itself in the widest sense of that term.

* This requirement also applies to group accounts drawn up under Schedule 4A. In addition the accounts of banking and insurance companies and groups drawn up under Schedules 9 and 9A must make the same disclosure. There is an exemption for small and medium-sized companies and for certain small and medium-sized groups.

This Opinion by Mary Arden QC (now the Honourable Mrs Justice Arden) forms an appendix to the UK Accounting Standards Board's 'Foreword to Accounting Standards' of June 1993. It is reprinted here by kind permission of the Accounting Standards Board.

Appendix V

UK's Urgent Issues Task Force Abstract 7 (dated 17 December 1992): 'true and fair view override disclosures' (1992)

THE ISSUE

1. The Companies Act 1985, as amended ('the Act') provides, both for individual company accounts and for group accounts, that if in special circumstances compliance with any of the provisions of the Act as to the matters to be included in a company's accounts (or notes thereto) is inconsistent with the requirement to give a true and fair view of the state of affairs and profit or loss, the directors shall depart from that provision to the extent necessary to give a true and fair view. Where this true and fair view override is used the Act requires that 'particulars of any such departure, the reasons for it and its effect shall be given in a note to the accounts.' The Act gives no further elaboration of this requirement.

2. The objectives of this disclosure requirement are to highlight instances where there are departures from specific rules in the Act and to provide the reader of the accounts with information on the position had the normal rules in the Act been applied. This is necessary in order to assist in achieving the equivalence of information available in respect of companies not only in the UK and Ireland but throughout the European Community.

3. The interpretation of the requirement in practice has varied and there has been a tendency for some companies to understate rather than emphasise the significance of what they have done. In some cases it has not been clear from the notes to the accounts whether the directors consider that they have departed from a specific statutory rule and that the true and fair view override is being invoked.

UITF CONSENSUS

4. The Task Force reached a consensus that in cases where the true and fair view override is being invoked this should be stated clearly

and unambiguously. To this end the statutory disclosure requirement should be interpreted as follows:-

(a) 'Particulars of any such departure' – a statement of the treatment which the Act would normally require in the circumstances and a description of the treatment actually adopted;

(b) 'the reasons for it' – a statement as to why the treatment prescribed would not give a true and fair view;

(c) 'its effect' – a description of how the position shown in the accounts is different as a result of the departure, normally with quantification, except (i) where quantification is already evident in the accounts themselves (an example of which might be a presentation rather than a measurement matter, such as an adaptation of the headings in the Act's format requirements not covered by paragraph 3(3) of Schedule 4), or (ii) whenever the effect cannot reasonably be quantified, in which case the directors should explain the circumstances.

5. Where a departure continues in subsequent financial statements, the disclosures should be made in all such subsequent statements, and should include corresponding amounts for the previous year.

6. Where a departure affects only the corresponding amounts, the disclosures required by this abstract should be given for those corresponding amounts.

7. The disclosures required by this abstract should either be included, or cross-referenced, in the note required under paragraph 36A of Schedule 4 (re: compliance with accounting standards and particulars of any material departure from those standards and the reasons for it).

8. The expression 'particulars of any such departure, the reasons for it and its effect' is also used in paragraph 15 of Schedule 4 and paragraph 22 of Schedule 9 (both relating to departure from the specified statutory accounting principles) and paragraph 3(2) of Schedule 4A (use of inconsistent accounting rules for an undertaking included in group accounts). The interpretation of the expression given in this abstract is also applicable to these cases.

DATE FROM WHICH EFFECTIVE

9. The interpretation required by this abstract should be adopted in financial statements relating to accounting periods ending on or after 23 December 1992.

REFERENCES

Companies Act 1985, sections 226(5) and 227(6), Schedule 4 paragraphs 15 and 36A, Schedule 4A paragraph 3(2) and Schedule 9 paragraph 22.

Northern Ireland – Companies (Northern Ireland) Order 1986 articles 234(5) and 235(6), Schedule 4 paragraphs 15 and 36A and Schedule 4A paragraph 3(2), and Companies (1986 Order) (Bank Accounts) Regulations (NI) 1992 (SR 1992/258), Schedule 1 paragraph 22.

Republic of Ireland – Companies (Amendment) Act 1986 sections 3(1) (d)–(e), and 6, European Communities (Companies: Group Accounts) Regulations 1992 regulations 14(3)–(4) and 29 (2)–(3), and European Communities (Credit Institutions: Accounts) Regulations 1992 (SI No. 294 of 1992), the Schedule, Chapter 2, paragraph 22. There is no equivalent reference to paragraph 36A of Schedule 4 to the Act.